THE ART OF
CREATIVE THINKING

biography

Rod Judkins is an artist, writer and lecturer. After gaining an MA at the Royal College of Art he had numerous one-man exhibitions of his paintings. His best-selling book, *Change Your Mind: 57 Ways to Unlock Your Creative Self*, has been translated into many languages. He has lectured on creative thinking at Central Saint Martins College of Art for fifteen years. His workshops and lectures demonstrate how creativity can be of practical benefit to individuals, companies and businesses in any field.

www.rodjudkins.com

Twitter:@rodjudkins

rodjudkins@hotmail.com

THE ART OF
CREATIVE THINKING

rod judkins

SCEPTRE

First published in Great Britain in 2015 by Sceptre
An imprint of Hodder & Stoughton
An Hachette UK company

First published in paperback in 2016

4

A CIP catalogue record for this title is
available from the British Library

Paperback ISBN 978 1 444 79449 6
eBook ISBN 978 1 444 79447 2

Illustrations © Rod Judkins

Typeset by Hewer Text UK Ltd, Edinburgh
Printed and bound by Clays Ltd, St Ives plc

Hodder & Stoughton policy is to use papers that are
natural, renewable and recyclable products and made
from wood grown in sustainable forests. The logging and
manufacturing processes are expected to conform to the
environmental regulations of the country of origin.

Hodder & Stoughton Ltd
Carmelite House
50 Victoria Embankment
London EC4Y 0DZ

www.sceptrebooks.co.uk

For Zelda, Scarlet and Louis

introduction

When I first stepped into an art college as a student, I instantly felt at home – for the first time ever.

At school, creativity was suppressed and crushed. It was something that teachers and authorities actually feared. They regarded it as dangerous, something they couldn't control. They steered students away from it in the same way they steered them away from drugs, burglary or gambling.

At art college I found the opposite. The spirit was one in which mistakes were good. Where you could try and fail. There was no emphasis on getting it 'right'. All around me were people experimenting for the sheer hell of it, doing things that made no sense – or rather doing things *because* they made no sense. There was an air of freedom and release. While all around in the world outside people were being thoughtlessly reasonable, doing something because it was what everyone else was doing. Paradoxically, the creative thinking of art college led to more worthwhile accomplishments than the logical, sensible approach. Many years later when I returned to art education as a university lecturer I found the environment to be the same.

Since emerging from art college all those years ago I've balanced various roles – as an educator, artist, writer, adviser and speaker – and have also become a hunter-gatherer of creative techniques. After leaving the Royal College of Art I had numerous solo exhibitions of my paintings. I have exhibited in many countries, and also at Tate Britain, the Royal Academy and National Portrait Gallery. I've taught at Central Saint Martins College of Art since 1999 and am also a creative consultant, working with companies and businesses around the world, delivering workshops that solve professional problems using creativity as the key. The workshops reveal useful techniques that access original ideas and help people and businesses develop a more direct relationship to their own creativity.

I care passionately about taking the spirit of creativity that exists in the art world out into the wider world. I didn't write *The Art of Creative Thinking* because I wanted to. I wrote it because it was needed. In my many years helping students, businesses and companies across various industries and people in all fields, from scientists to office workers, I have seen first-hand how thinking creatively can transform everyday life. I've shown how the principles of jazz improvisation could make an admin office run more smoothly, how to help an entrepreneur whose scuba-diving company was facing bankruptcy because sharks had infested the area (long story short: we made this his unique selling point) and helped a company to sell their designer furniture by promoting it as uncomfortable.

This book is intended to be an overview of many useful creative-thinking techniques, and an examination of the thought processes and methods creative people use and which can be used to help everyone. But I also want to share stories of some of the inevitable obstacles that aspiring creative thinkers encounter and the methods they use to overcome them. These are challenges that all of us face in day-to-day life, whatever our career or field of expertise: anxiety that we have no special talents; the absence of any burning, driving passion; craving success in an area we're not actually any good at; being unable to make a living from our true passion; having too many other responsibilities and commitments; feeling either too young or too old, too naïve or too jaded.

This book is not meant to be read in a linear way. When your creativity is running low or you feel the need for inspiration, open it at any page at random.

The Art of Creative Thinking began as a tribute to what all of us can learn from art school, but what I hope to show more than anything is that thinking creatively is not a *professional* activity – it's a way of relating to your life. Creativity is not about creating a painting, novel or house but creating *yourself*, creating a better future and taking the opportunities that you are currently missing.

see what happens when you make something happen

The surrealist artist Salvador Dalí was featured on an American game show called *What's My Line?*, in which blindfolded celebrity panellists interrogated a 'mystery guest' in order to guess their occupation. The panel posed their questions but became confused almost immediately, as Dalí answered 'Yes' to almost every question. They asked him if he was a writer and he answered 'Yes'. It was true; as well as three non-fiction books Dalí had written a novel, *Hidden Faces*. Asked if he was a performer: 'Yes.' He had produced many pieces of performance art. At one point an exasperated panellist exclaimed, 'There's nothing this man doesn't do!'

A creative mind wants to shape the world around it. On *What's My Line?* Dalí could have said he was a furniture maker; he designed many chairs and his sofa of Mae West's lips became a design classic. As a film-maker he created the groundbreaking *Un Chien Andalou* and *L'Âge d'Or*. He also masterminded the ethereal dream sequence in Hitchcock's *Spellbound* and the unique short animated film *Destino* with Walt Disney. As a jewellery maker he created intricate jewellery designs that often contained moving parts, such as the Royal Heart. Made of gold and encrusted with rubies and diamonds, its centre beat like a real heart. As an architect he designed buildings, the most famous being his house in Port Lligat and his extraordinary Teatro Museo in Figueres. He wanted a house, so he made one – why get someone else to do it? He also designed theatre sets, clothes, textiles and perfume bottles. The manufacturer of Chupa Chups lollipops (still in stores today) asked Dalí to design a new logo. He created a daisy insignia and lettering (still in use today). He even suggested the logo be on top of the wrapper so that it was always fully displayed – advice the manufacturer followed. Dalí could have thought, 'I'm a famous, wealthy surrealist artist who has a place in the history of art', but he didn't; it sounded like fun so he gave it a go. He didn't have any rules in his head about what was important or unimportant. Dalí even created a person – often referred to as Dalí's Frankenstein – Amanda Lear. He met her in a nightclub in 1965 when she was called Peki d'Oslo. Dalí renamed her, remade her and spread mysterious stories about her, successfully launching her into the disco/art scene, which she then took by storm.

School and society make us feel our abilities are limited and rob us of our creative confidence. Although we are born with incredible imagination, intuition and intelligence, many people are trained not to use these powers, and as a result they wither. Our schools, families and friends project a limited view of our abilities onto us. If the creative want something, they go ahead and try. Not all of Dalí's designs, films and experiments in different mediums were a success, but enough worked for him to become respected.

Modern designers like Philippe Starck and Zaha Hadid also have a unique vision. They are famous for designing iconic opera houses, stadiums and hotels. They also design cars, bicycles, lamps, jewellery, chairs and boats. They developed a way of thinking that could be applied to any project. Sometimes you succeed and sometimes you fail but it's important to try everything and see what happens.

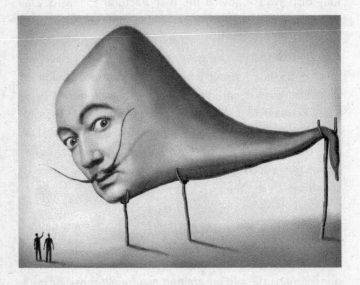

A creative mindset can be applied to everything you do and enrich every aspect of your life. Creativity isn't a switch that's flicked on or off; it's a way of seeing, engaging with and responding to the world around you. The creative are creative when filing documents, cooking, arranging timetables or doing housework. Try to develop an alternative way of thinking that can be applied to any challenge or project, no matter how far out of your comfort zone.

'I think any actor worth their salt wants to show as much versatility as they possibly can.'

Daniel Radcliffe

Agree? Venture beyond your comfort zone in the next chapter.
Disagree? Discover why creativity and tidiness just don't go on p. 173.

be a beginner, for ever

I had to create a new TV soap. I'd never done anything like that before. I was an artist, a painter, yet here I found myself, standing in front of thirty TV professionals. They were looking at me impatiently and expectantly.

I didn't know what I was in for when I accepted the job. The Dubai TV station had asked me to deliver creative workshops that I had developed for my students at Central Saint Martins. CSM made them available to a wider audience. The TV station flew me to Dubai and showered me with luxury: a room in the Dubai Hilton, a driver and limo, expenses, the works. I felt obligated to them and had prepared thoroughly. I didn't want to go all that way and discover I'd left out something important.

They had rented a conference room in a five-star hotel for me to deliver my workshop. As I was led in to meet the production team, the manager turned to me and said, 'Oh, by the way, instead of the workshops, we'd like you to help us create a new soap based in Dubai.' It was a bombshell. My preparation was wasted.

I stood in front of the eager production team. The room oozed wealth and opulence; embroidered tablecloths, ornate chairs and hi-tech screens everywhere. I felt ill at ease. I was used to art studios with paint spatters on the walls, bare floors and a place where you could make mistakes with freedom. I gave a short talk about myself; in reality I was stalling for time, trying to work out what to do. I knew I couldn't produce anything creative in the room, yet they'd spent a fortune on it. I'd have to disrupt it. To the dismay of the hotel staff, I made them move all the tables and chairs out. I didn't want everyone sitting down feeling relaxed. With the room empty, I felt better. It was like a blank canvas to an artist or blank sheet of paper to a writer. They all looked irritated, though.

The TV station were struggling to create a new soap opera because their ideas were predictable and dull. They wanted me to resurrect them. I said it would be easier to scrap their ideas and start fresh. Better to think new ideas than waste time trying to salvage old ones. They were annoyed by this.

The team of scriptwriters, cameramen, production staff, soundmen, set designers, costume designers and more had attitudes that stifled creative thinking: 'I have been doing this for years. I'm an expert. I have been trained to do this properly, I know exactly what I'm doing.' They wanted to do things the way they had always done them. I knew I couldn't work with them until they opened their minds to new methods.

I swapped their roles. I asked the cameramen to write some script ideas, the costume designers to write up characters, the soundmen to think of locations and so on. They were furious.

I had to convince them to give it a try. Eventually they opened up and had a go. Fear of failure vanished because the weight of expectation had been lifted. They no longer had a reputation to protect because they were not doing what they'd been trained to do. They improvised. They played around. New, original ideas poured out. They had fun. They were liberated. We created some new scripts with exciting characters, unusual settings and innovative plot lines. They wanted to get actors to rehearse the roles and start filming 'properly'. I pointed out that that was what they usually did. Instead we filmed a rough episode with them acting the roles. They ad-libbed unusual and interesting ideas as we filmed.

They developed the rough ideas further after I'd returned to England. The soap went on air. It was unique and completely different for Dubai. The process determined the end result.

Make the most of inexperience. A beginner has a fresh perspective. The amateurish and unprofessional are open to new ideas: they'll try anything. They don't know how things 'should' be done, and haven't yet become entrenched in a particular method. Nothing is 'wrong' for them because they don't know what is 'right'.

It's important to avoid becoming an expert, specialist or authority. An expert constantly refers to *past* experience. Whatever has worked in the past, they repeat. They turn knowledge into a repetitive ritual. Their expertise becomes a straitjacket. Furthermore, experts claim to have many years' experience. What they actually have is one year's experience repeated many times. They see new methods as a threat to their expertise, and seek to stamp them out.

To breathe fresh air into yourself or your company, spend a day working on something that's valuable, but not what you're 'supposed' to be working on. Switching jobs creates an environment that encourages innovation. Constantly search for new ways of doing the same things and do not repeat what you already know. Don't do things in the usual way; do them in the unusual way.

'Whatever I know how to do, I've already done. Therefore I must always do what I do not know how to do.'

Eduardo Chillida

Inspired? *Discover the self-taught architect on p. 77.*
Uninspired? *Imitate your idols on p. 195.*

blame Michelangelo

The cult of the creative genius appeared with art's first super-star, Michelangelo. In 1550 his biographer and PR guru, Vasari, promoted the idea of the 'Divine Michelangelo'. His talent was a gift from God, Vasari said, and claimed that God bestowed such ability only on the privileged few, the chosen ones. It fostered an elite and disempowering attitude to creativity.

What Vasari failed to mention was Michelangelo's reliance on an army of assistants. Archives contain hundreds of bills for his highly skilled helpers – a dozen worked continuously on the Sistine Chapel ceiling, for example, which explains the sheer scale of his achievement and the fact that this physical task might seem impossible. For me, this does not belittle his achievement. His role was similar to a film director, like Francis Ford Coppola in today's world, someone who realises an enormous project by guiding the technical crew to the fulfilment of that vision – an awesome achievement, but not a superhuman one. While the *Godfather* trilogy was Coppola's vision, and he got incredible performances out of Marlon Brando and the rest of the cast, it would be wrong to attribute the design of costumes, the writing of the script, arranging the lighting, the editing and everything else involved in the making of a film to the director.

Undoubtedly one of the world's great geniuses, Michelangelo had not so much a divine gift as an intensely nurtured talent. Brought up by quarrymen, he could chisel and cut blocks of stone from the age of six. By the age of twelve he had been carving stone for thousands of hours. At fourteen he was apprenticed to an artist's studio. That level of skilled training is not possible today. In fact, it's illegal.

The old masters are a great source of inspiration, but we cannot ever emulate their level of skill. We have to discover our own strengths. When I deliver creativity workshops to companies I try to get everyone to take part: the account-ants, admin staff, technicians, whoever is around, not just the 'creatives'. By the end of the sessions the 'non-creatives' are surprised at how creative they are. They had been led to believe they didn't have the ability and therefore lacked the confidence. Creative thinking is like a muscle that needs to be strengthened through exercise. I often set exercises that each last five or ten minutes, rather as an athlete might do a series of short workouts to get fit.

How often have you heard, 'I can't draw to save my life' or 'I'm tone-deaf'? The concept of innate talent erodes confidence. Many people do not develop their talents because they are made to feel they weren't born with the amount required to be professional.

'Talent' is often confused with 'innate ability', then, but many people also confuse 'talent' with 'skill'. A modern creative mind does not aim to display technical proficiency or mastery; it is more concerned with communicating ideas and concepts in whatever medium is suitable. It's more interesting if an engineer builds a rocket from rocks, a painter paints with blood or a harpist plays a washing line. Our task is to develop our creative potential whatever forms it may take, whether we think we were 'born' with it or not.

'Not every person has the same kinds of talents, so you discover what yours are and work with them.'

Frank Gehry

Convinced? *Discover what the Fab Four can tell you about talent versus effort on p. 25.*
Not convinced? *See if Picasso can persuade you on p. 198.*

be the medium of your medium

Did Space Shuttle *Columbia* break apart while re-entering the Earth's atmosphere, instantly killing all seven crew members, because of a poorly designed PowerPoint slide? During the launch, a few days earlier, a piece of insulation foam had struck the shuttle's wing. While *Columbia* was still orbiting the Earth, NASA engineers showed the results of their investigation to their superiors. The piece of foam was hundreds of times bigger than anything they had ever tested and could have caused a severe fracture. Unfortunately their warning was conveyed on PowerPoint. Their superiors walked away from the presentation thinking everything was fine.

Visually stunning presentations tell a story, engage their audience and make information meaningful, entertaining and beautiful. The sheer magnitude of the problem NASA was facing was lost. It was buried in a slide crowded with bullet points. Edward Tufte, a Yale University professor and researcher into the presentation of visual information, investigated the incident and demonstrated that PowerPoint encouraged poor thinking by its very design. He criticised the format: complex ideas squashed into bulleted lists distort the information. If it had been presented in another medium, the disaster could almost certainly have been prevented. An independent board reached the same conclusion after reading Tufte's analysis, admitting that: 'It is easy to understand how a senior manager might read this PowerPoint slide and not realise that it addresses a life-threatening situation.'

Your working environment, whether it's a supermarket, office, studio or building site, persuades you to work and think in certain ways. The more aware you are of that, and the more you understand your medium, the more you can use it to your advantage. A meeting about finance is not about finance, it's about meetings: their format, internal politics, hierarchies and the way things are managed and governed. The most common decision at a meeting is to have another meeting. That's not really a decision.

Artists were the first to investigate this idea, in particular the surrealists. René Magritte's paintings were paintings about paintings. His surrealist ideas have had a profound influence on our understanding of how the medium transforms the message. Instead of producing art about something he had observed, his work reflected on what a painting was and the actual effect that it has on the viewer. He asked his audience to doubt the illusion they were presented with.

Magritte's painting The Treachery of Images showed a pipe with the words 'This is not a pipe' underneath. This seems at first glance to be a contradiction, but is actually true: it is not a pipe, it is an image of a pipe. Magritte was pointing out that a painting is an illusion. He was trying to understand the language of painting, how it worked and how it conveyed ideas, and to challenge observers' preconditioned perceptions of the art form. A painting of flowers is not about flowers, it is about the medium of painting: the traditions, history, the frame, the gallery and the expectations the viewer has.

Artists like Magritte understood their medium and conveyed information that was visual poetry. That made it more memorable and easily understood, unlike the information from posters, television, newspapers and the Internet that we're bombarded with now. We're drowning in it. We are dazed by PowerPoint presentations in which multiple bullet points are fired at us. Bullet points that can kill.

Most people are passive consumers who never analyse the medium. In a cinema, the public go along with the illusion and enjoy the spectacle. For a creative thinker the entertainment is in deconstructing the spectacle and analysing how they could have structured the film differently. What if the last scene and the first scene were swapped round? What if the lead and supporting actor changed roles? What if it was a silent movie? Imagining how the elements could be altered sharpens creative thinking. To flourish in any field of activity you need to gain a deep understanding of it.

'The new media are not bridges between man and nature: they are nature.'

Marshall McLuhan

Not the medium of your medium? *Be your subject instead, from the inside out, on p. 58.*

Not the medium of your medium? *Be your subject instead, from the inside out, on p. 58.*

don't be someone else

'In order to be irreplaceable one must always be different,' said eccentric, pioneering French designer Coco Chanel. From the beginning of her career Chanel defied convention. She didn't like the way women were forced to be uncomfortable to look fashionable. She didn't like corsets, so she replaced them with casual elegance and comfort. She was heavily attacked by the fashion press, but was unrepentant: 'Luxury must be comfortable, otherwise it is not luxury.' Her new vision made her one of the most important figures in the history of fashion. In the nineteen-twenties and thirties she popularised sporty, casual chic. Her little black dresses and trademark suits were timeless designs that are still popular today. People laughed at the way she dressed but that was the secret of her success: she didn't look like anyone else. 'The most courageous act is still to think for yourself. Aloud,' she said. Her first success was a dress she fashioned out of an old jersey on a chilly day. Many people asked where she'd bought it. Her response was to offer to make one for them. 'My fortune is built on that old jersey that I'd put on because it was cold in

Deauville,' she said. Chanel's work radiates with her defiance to be completely herself.

Like Chanel, you have to make the most of your uniqueness. Nobody else can draw from your childhood and teenage experiences, from your schooldays, or from your parents.

Everyone is searching for originality. Ironically, it is right there within them, but most people are too busy being someone else. Creative people are prepared to be themselves. They make the most of their own experiences,

whether good or bad. The advantage of being themselves is that they are original. There is no one like them. This makes whatever they do unique.

Artist Tracey Emin has pulled down the barrier most people keep between their public self and their real self by using her own experiences as subject matter. Her poetic artworks consist of intimate objects most people would not consider showing in public: her unmade, dirty bed with stained sheets, a packet of cigarettes her uncle was holding when decapitated in a car crash and a tent appliquéd with the names of everyone she had ever slept with. She is uncompromisingly herself.

We spend much of our lives not being who we really are. There are huge pressures on everyone to be someone else; to live up to others' expectations – to be a perfect parent, obedient employee, selfless partner or high-achieving son or daughter. We lose the ability to be good at being ourselves, and we forget who we are. The world is pushing constantly to submerge you in orthodoxy, to make you indistinguishable from everybody else. To fight against it is to be involved in a lifelong struggle.

To be successfully creative you have to realise it's OK to be yourself. We all have weaknesses and strengths; the creative accept them and use them both. The biggest benefit you can be to your company, school, business or family is to accentuate what is special and unique about yourself. That's difficult in a society that puts huge emphasis on conformity.

Everyone needs to analyse and understand what makes them tick, like taking a clock apart to discover how it works. Self-knowledge will help you to understand what you have to offer that's special. Ask yourself, What is the best idea I've ever had? How did it come about? When am I at my most creative? Nurture your individual approach and personality. It is more important to be the best version of yourself than a bad copy of someone else.

'To be nobody but yourself in a world which is doing its best, night and day, to make you everybody else means to fight the hardest battle which any human being can fight; and never stop fighting.'

e.e. cummings

More? See why James Joyce benefitted from being self-indulgent on p. 149, but why it had the opposite effect on his own daughter on p. 165.

be a generator

An actor instinctively disliked auditions because his fate was in others' hands. He realized it was better to create a role and not wait for a director to give him one. He found an interesting book about a boxer that he thought could be turned into a film, with him playing the lead role. He carried it around with him and showed it to everyone. He persuaded a film producer to finance a film based on the book. The producer had one condition: that director Martin Scorsese came on board. Scorsese wasn't interested, though – he didn't like boxing and the book wasn't about a significant, champion fighter. This boxer's only talent was absorbing punishment. After months of persuasion however, Scorsese became intrigued by the boxer's fight with his inner demons and agreed. The film went into production. The actor was Robert De Niro and the book was *Raging Bull*. It was the life story of a boxer called Jake La Motta. De Niro gained sixty pounds to portray La Motta in his post-boxing years, an extraordinary commitment, and *Raging Bull* went on to become one of the most critically acclaimed films of all time and to win De Niro the Academy Award for Best Actor.

To produce anything worthwhile, you have to be proactive and generate it, not sit around and wait. Most people sleep-walk through life, never asking themselves what they're doing, why, or if it really matters to them. They absorb the values of their culture, parents and friends, and then accept them unquestioningly.

One of my creativity workshop participants was an actor with an interest in Shakespeare. He was attending endless auditions but wasn't getting any roles. We analysed his predicament. He needed the approval of theatre direc-tors to pass the auditions. Why not become your own theatre director? I suggested. Put on the play yourself? No money for other actors? Play all the roles yourself. No props? Make them yourself out of cardboard boxes. He became a one-man Shakespeare company. He staged *Hamlet* and played all the parts. His shows were unique, fascinating and unexpected. He became such a huge success he was offered parts in Broadway plays. He turned them down. Why go back to being at the mercy of others' decisions?

The principle applies to everyone. Do you think interde-partmental communication could be better where you work? Then instigate a solution. Do you want to be a writer? Stop sitting waiting for your big idea – just start writing.

We come alive when we're generating something we consider worthwhile. The creative drive on with the projects that matter to them. If they feel what they're doing is of real significance they devote all their energy and time to it. Doing what matters is what matters.

'The least of things with a meaning is worth more in life than the greatest of things without it.'

Carl Jung

Agree? *Discover how Salvador Dalí made things happen on p. 4.*
Disagree? *See why money matters just as much as anything else on p. 180.*

be committed to commitment

I had never been so petrified. I didn't understand what was happening. I was a child of seven and I clung to my aunt's jacket for fear of being swept away in the stampeding mob of screaming, wailing girls. The noise was deafening. It's impossible to describe the sheer magnitude of the hysteria. Girls fainted and collapsed and ambulance men rushed past holding their floppy, contorted bodies. It was like a medieval battlefield. I was crushed on all sides by a throng of thousands. Their eyes were wet with tears and their faces twisted with distress.

Then the Beatles stepped out of the plane and things went really crazy. It was 1964 and my aunt, who worked at Heathrow, had taken me to see the Fab Four return to England after a triumphant trip to the USA.

When the Beatles played on the legendary *Ed Sullivan Show* on TV it was a milestone in American pop culture. A record-breaking audience of 73 million viewers were mesmerised.

To the USA, the Beatles were an overnight success, but in fact Lennon and McCartney had been playing together since 1957. In the clubs of Hamburg they performed/endured live non-stop shows for eight hours a day, seven days a week until two o'clock in the morning, and had to work incredibly hard to attract audiences from the many clubs in Hamburg competing for attention. Their abilities and confidence increased. By 1964 they had played roughly 1,200 times, totalling thousands of hours' playing time, more than most rock bands play in their entire careers. Those hours of performing set the Beatles apart. They were addicted to practice, yet their rehearsing was not repetitive but adventurous. They didn't play the classic rock songs of the time over and over until they sounded exactly like the originals, as other bands did; they experimented and improvised, constantly embellishing the

standards until they made them their own. They understood that there was nothing to be gained from mechanical repetition. The Beatles gave each other constant feedback, to improve and make their sound more and more like the Beatles and less and less like everyone else.

In their early days the Beatles were not great musicians; there were better, more technically proficient guitarists, singers and drummers (John Lennon was once asked at a press conference if he thought Ringo was the best drummer in the world; he jokingly replied, 'Ringo isn't the best drummer in the Beatles.'). Yet on *The Ed Sullivan Show*, the four lads from the backstreets of Liverpool displayed no trace of nerves. Their confidence was the result of their years of playing together and painstaking development.

Ninety-nine per cent of the difference between successful innovative people and those who fail is commitment to self-improvement. The extraordinary amount of time and effort the successful put into developing their work amplifies their abilities. If someone is more successful than you, the chances are they work harder at self-development. Practice is important but it has to be *good* practice. Bad practice is thoughtlessly repeating something to perfect it. Good practice is putting time into imaginative improvement. When Matisse produced a series of paintings of the same female model, he didn't achieve more and more accuracy: he achieved more and more inventiveness.

The Beatles got the most out of their talent by investing the imaginative practice needed to develop their qualities. We only get out what we put in. No masterpieces have ever been produced by a talented but lazy artist. People who become rich enough to never need to work again are the people who never stop working.

'A genius! For thirty-seven years I've practised fourteen hours a day, and now they call me a genius!'

Pablo de Sarasate

Discover how two of the twentieth century's most accomplished musicians overcame unimaginable challenges on p. 263, or why, like Beethoven, you should look forward to disappointment on p. 187.

be positive about negatives

Roy Lichtenstein established a reputation as an abstract expressionist painter in the nineteen-fifties when it was the dominant style. He produced large, splashy paintings full of dribbles and splatters – standard for the time. His painting was respected and his exhibitions did moderately well. Reviews were reasonable. He swam with the stream.

Suddenly, in 1961, he changed direction overnight. He discarded abstraction and began making large paintings copied from comic-book illustrations. His new work was hard-edged, brash, flat and expressionless, traced from enlarged images. It was the result of a challenge from his young son, who pointed to a Mickey Mouse comic book and said, 'I bet you can't paint as good as that, eh, Dad?' So Lichtenstein enlarged and copied one of the illustrations exactly onto canvas.

Lichtenstein's friends hated it. It was their first encounter with Pop Art. They had never seen anything like it. It was the opposite of the emotionally intense abstract expressionist paintings they were used to. Comic-book illustrations were worthless, shallow trash in their eyes, symbolising the worst of American commercialism.

It was the strongest reaction a piece of Lichtenstein's work had ever received. He realised it was better to have a powerful response, even if negative, than the respectful yet muted response he was used to. He produced more comic-book paintings, exhibited them, and the critics savaged them. Again, Lichtenstein reasoned that although negative, at least he was achieving a strong reaction. Eventually his iconic Pop Art, comic-book style struck a chord with the younger members of the art world and cemented his place in the history of art.

If others respond strongly to something you've done, that's positive – even if the reaction is negative. What should concern you more than anything is no reaction whatsoever. The history of culture is one of negativity towards new work and new ideas, to a point where public annoyance can be seen as an endorsement. To be a successful person you often have to create a strong foundation with the bricks others throw at you.

'The only thing worse than being talked about is not being talked about.'

Oscar Wilde

Convinced? *Meet James Dyson, the inventor who just wouldn't give up, on p. 69.*
Not convinced? *Meet a pair of guitarists who took advantage of a disadvantage on p. 141 – one lost his memory, the other his fingers.*

be practically useless

The Juicy Salif is a lemon squeezer that doesn't work. Yet it's also a design icon and a huge commercial success. Why?

The design consists of a teardrop body supported by three legs, cast from aluminium, a metal that we associate with modernity and aircraft. What makes it so distinctive and therefore so popular is that it is imbued with the personality of its creator, Philippe Starck. It brings together all his obsessions. It's been exhibited in New York's Museum of Modern Art, so it's not just design, but art.

Starck designed the Juicy Salif in a restaurant while eating squid. He squeezed lemon over the squid, wondered if the shape of the squid could be used as the basis for a lemon squeezer and started sketching on a napkin (now on permanent display in Milan's Alessi museum).

Creative thinkers care about their work because it's full of the things they care about. As a child Starck was fascinated by science-fiction comics and spent hours redrawing spaceships. His father was an aircraft designer and Starck was enthralled by the sleek lines of the aluminium craft. Another of his obsessions was the diverse shapes of animals and plants. He poured all these disparate influences into the design of the lemon squeezer. The result was successful *because* it was personal. He didn't ask chefs and cooks to test prototypes of the Juicy Salif and adapt it to their needs. He made it the way he wanted. One of the key ingredients of the success of the Juicy Salif was that it didn't work. Its height made it unstable, lemon juice dribbled down the legs and its feet scratched kitchen work surfaces. You might expect this to detract from its reputation, but no, it enhanced it. The public identified with the view that expression was more

important than function and that it's the idea that counts. The fact that it was dysfunctional became its unique selling point.

The genuinely innovative are led by their passions and not by rational ambitions. New ideas spring from personal interests, even if they seem irrelevant to the task at hand. Innovative people have to put practical considerations to one side because thinking about logistics leads to thinking logically, which ties down the leaps of the mind required to create something unique.

A counterpoint to the orthodoxy of 'form follows function' was the 'Well Tempered Chair', a design icon produced by Ron Arad. It makes the sitter bad-tempered because it's made from sheets of steel and is too uncomfortable to sit on. The infamous fashion designer Alexander McQueen designed shoes that were impossible to walk in and clothes that couldn't be worn. Architects Renzo Piano and Richard Rogers designed the Pompidou Centre in Paris inside out. Utilitarian features such as escalators, lifts, plumbing, pipes, air vents and electrical cables were put on the outside, freeing up space inside for exhibitions and events. The futuristic design led to spiralling maintenance costs because it required constant repainting. All these creative thinkers poured their obsessions into their work and ignored the practicalities.

To be true to an idea, you have to value expression over perfection, vitality over finish, movement over the static, and form over function. Put your personality before practicality and your individuality into everything. Ironing out impracticalities irons out what is unique.

'It's the addicts that stay with it. They're not necessarily the most talented, they're just the ones that can't get it out of their systems.'

Harold Brown

Now meet the most famous example of imperfection in the world on p. 65.

don't think about what others think about

The astrophysicist Subrahmanyan Chandrasekhar loved his subject. His ideas were so strange that other scientists didn't accept them for years. He worked in relative obscurity. He came up with the model for stellar evolution that became the basis for the theory of black holes. He also was remarkable in another way.

At the University of Chicago Chandrasekhar was scheduled to teach a class in astrophysics, eighty miles away from the main campus at the astrological observatory. He was looking forward to it, but only two students signed up. The embarrassingly low attendance was a joke among Chandrasekhar's colleagues. Lecturers pride themselves on popular classes with high attendance. Chandrasekhar was expected to cancel the class because he had to commute the 160 miles along back-country roads for just two students. But he didn't, because he enjoyed the subject and the classes. He and the two students threw ideas around. They were engrossed in their subject – motivated by the enjoyment of their ideas and fuelled by the satisfaction of creating new ways to describe reality. Their fulfilment came from the thrill of reaching new perceptions. It was the smallest class in the history of university education, and was mocked and ridiculed.

A few years later both of the two students won the Nobel Prize for physics. Later still Chandrasekhar himself was awarded a Nobel Prize, also for physics. They had the last laugh. It became the most successful university class of all time. Everyone in the class had won a Nobel Prize.

Don't be distracted by the views of others: focus on what engages and inspires you. The most exhilarating experiences are generated in the mind, triggered by information that challenges our thinking. If it's not fun there's no point in doing it.

If you're excited by a subject that no one else is, all that should matter to you is that you're interested. Revolutionary thinkers who create totally new ideas are driven by their interests, not whether or not others are as interested.

'I swear to God, if I were a piano player or an actor or something and all those dopes thought I was terrific, I'd hate it. I wouldn't even want them to clap for me. People always clap for the wrong things.'

J.D. Salinger

Disagree? See why others' opinions of you can be worth more than you may think in the next chapter.
Agree? Meet Ed Wood, the zealous film-maker who was so woefully bad he won awards, on p. 113.

be perceptive about perception

The great nineteenth-century engineer Isambard Kingdom Brunel is remembered for railways, bridges and the first propeller-driven steamships. Yet his most innovative construction was his image. The famous photograph of Brunel standing before the launching chains of the *Great Eastern* created an idea of Brunel as a romantic genius, arrogantly relaxed and confident. Although it looks like a snapshot of an insouciant savant taking a break, it was actually a painstaking act of image manipulation.

This classic 'snapshot' in fact took several days to construct. In the other photos taken on the shoot, although artfully posed, Brunel appears hesitant, insignificant, balding, conservative and inconsequential against the backdrop of huge chains and ships. Yet one photo struck the right note.

Both the photographer and Brunel were searching for an *idealised* image. In the eighteen-fifties snapshots weren't possible; taking photos outdoors was arduous and extremely time-consuming. It required a huge amount of equipment including a portable darkroom with an arsenal of toxic chemicals. Brunel had many demanding projects requiring his time at this point, but he ignored them all because he appreciated the importance of the photograph. Brunel understood the effect the photo would have on public awareness of him and therefore his work.

The photographer took many photos over several days, and eventually they hit on the magic image that is cemented in the public's imagination. The photographer understood that the purpose of the photograph is not to reproduce reality but to create a new reality of the same intensity.

It's impossible to look at Brunel's engineering without his image in that photograph of him as a genius coming to mind. Brunel arguably owes his legacy and place in history to that photographer more than he does his engineering works.

Be aware of how your audience perceive and understand things, and appreciate that the aura created around a person, place or work affects how people respond to them. To get audiences to take your work seriously, it's necessary to get them to take *you* seriously. Sometimes, to convince people of the worth of your work, you have to convince them of *your* worth.

'We can control our lives by controlling our perceptions.'

Bruce Lipton

Not interested in improving your own image? *Consider becoming anonymous on p. 204 or discover the benefits of being as annoying as possible on p. 244.*

doubt everything all the time

Richard Feynman doubted traditional mathematics. That's a pretty big doubt. He created a new maths called Feynman diagrams (technically a new kind of algebra). Doubt was central to the thinking of Feynman, a Nobel Prize-winning American, famous for his work on quantum mechanics and particle physics. He doubted the ability of traditional maths to describe this new subatomic world and therefore invented a new maths, now the most widely used in that field. People were using old maths to describe a new world and it didn't work. He doubted everything, constantly, because he realised that if we didn't have doubt, we would not have any new ideas. He believed that nothing was absolutely certain.

Freedom to doubt is the most important aspect of our culture. Doubt should be promoted in every organisation and company. Many fear the consequences of doubt but it is a door to new potential; being unsure gives you the chance to improve the situation. It is absurd to think that we can find out everything there is to know by listening to experts, parents and authorities without doubting or testing it for ourselves.

It's not just those who seek to revolutionise our understanding of particle physics, like Feynman, who can benefit from doubt. Henry Ford's Model T dominated the car market after he introduced it in 1908. He doubted the lengthy, traditional way in which cars were made and invented the assembly line that enabled cars to be built from the finest materials but cheaply. He doubted the expense of supplying a wide choice of colours; he famously said, 'Any customer can have a car painted any colour that he wants so long as it is black.'

After years of innovations, though, Ford became complacent and stopped doubting. He had no doubt that the Model T was all people needed. By the nineteen-twenties, consumers and competitors did start doubting it – why couldn't they have new cars in new colours? Ford nearly destroyed his own company. His son, Edsel, saved the day by doubting his father's strategy and finally Ford moved with the changing times.

Doubt is a key to unlocking new ideas. Einstein doubted Newton. Picasso doubted Michelangelo. Beethoven doubted Mozart. That's why they moved things forward. If Einstein had believed that Newton was right we would have no theory of relativity. If Picasso had believed in Michelangelo's view of the world he would not have developed cubism. It's essential to doubt everyone and to know that you don't know. Certainty is a convenient and easy way out of our discomfort. It is the mind's equivalent of fast food – to satisfy our hunger for answers with minimal effort. Doubt, on the other hand, is a great incentive for personal growth. To doubt, to not know, to ask questions, to err and to fail, is the best and only way to learn, grow, progress and move forward.

Doubt this book. Doubt what you know. It's important to listen to teachers and experts and seek out knowledge – but at the same time, doubt. The power of science and art is doubt. Everything that has been achieved over the last 500 years is because of doubt. It is by doubting that we come to investigate, and by investigating that we discover new ideas. Doubt everyone and everything all the time – especially yourself.

'Doubt is not a pleasant condition, but certainty is absurd.'

Voltaire

Still feeling sure of yourself? The next chapter should cure that.

feel inadequate

Do you feel inadequate, that you're not as talented as others? Good. Feeling inadequate is a driving force to do better. The self-satisfied are not the ones producing great things. They're sitting back feeling smug and conceited.

Over many years talking to and researching creative people, I've learned that self-doubt is an important motivator. When I was a student at the Royal College of Art, many famous people such as Ridley Scott, Henry Moore and Dennis Hopper used to visit to discover the new trends. I was always struck by their humility. I remember the students' surprise when David Bowie, who all of us were in awe of, was particularly insecure, regarding us as 'proper' and 'serious' artists and himself as a mere lightweight. The great creative minds are often racked with self-doubt but they turn it into a driving force, an engine that pushes them forward rather than something that holds them back. Because they feel inadequate they have to prove they are not. They do that by trying to do great things. Self-doubt and passion are a powerful combination.

The greatest artists suffer the greatest self-doubt. Many successful creative people, entrepreneurs, celebrities, artists and writers experience deep feelings of inadequacy – no matter what great successes they achieve.

'Sometimes I wake up in the morning before going off to a shoot, and I think, I can't do this; I'm a fraud. They're going to fire me – all these things. I'm fat; I'm ugly . . .' admitted the actress Kate Winslet, despite being the youngest person ever to acquire six Academy Award nominations and winning an Academy Award for Best Actress for *The Reader*. Traits such as having very high standards for yourself and your work are a factor in self-doubt. But setting yourself high standards is worthwhile.

Although he exuded self-confidence, John Lennon was surprisingly insecure and suffered from a deep lack of self-esteem. Lennon wrote the lyrics of the song 'Help' to express his confusion after the Beatles' meteoric rise to success: 'I was fat and depressed and I was crying out for help.' It was the first 'chink in the armour' of Lennon's self-protection. All his life, even when Beatlemania peaked, despite more number one singles and albums than any other group and breaking world records for concert attendances and television viewings, he still had poor self-esteem. It was the key force that drove him to do better and better.

Many successful creative people secretly worry that others will find out that they're not clever and capable. They expect the no-talent police to come and arrest them at any moment. They take little credit for their successes and attribute them to luck. But that is why they strive so hard. That's the kind of attitude they need to achieve great things. Self-doubt keeps them diligent. Without it, they wouldn't keep striving for higher standards. Fear of failure is a great motivator and it keeps the creative ego in check.

'I don't believe anyone ever suspects how completely unsure I am of my work and myself and what tortures of self-doubting the doubt of others has always given me.'

Tennessee Williams

More? *If you liked doubt, you'll love ignorance, on p. 128.*
Less? *If you've had enough of self-doubt for now, try p. 77.*

be naturally inspired

The structural strength and beauty of the bird's nest is remarkable, but how could it be used on a human scale? Architecture firm Herzog and de Meuron responded to this question by producing one of the most spectacular buildings of recent times, the 'Bird's Nest' Stadium, to be the centrepiece of the 2008 Beijing Olympics. The façade consists of thousands of steel 'twigs', in-filled with translucent panels with the same insulating qualities of mud, feathers and moss in a real bird's nest. The panels protect spectators from wind and rain but cleverly allow sunlight to seep through to feed the grass. The gaps in the façade allow natural ventilation because air flows through the public concourse and into the stadium, and eventually out through the holes in the roof.

The stadium achieved its aspiration to be a global landmark. The intoxicating beauty of the elliptical latticework shell is an aesthetic triumph that cemented China's reputation as the place for courageous creative risks. Even more impressive is that the radical structure tore up the rules of modernism that had become a kind of authoritarianism.

Whatever field you work in, nature can always provide you with new insights. Nature is creative by necessity. It is the consummate problem-solver. Animals, plants and microbes are skilled inventors and the ultimate engineers. After 3.8 billion years of evolution, they have found what works and, most importantly, what lasts. It has taken them millions of years to evolve solutions that we can access in minutes.

Innovation inspired by nature is more than just looking at patterns and structures – the shape of a dragonfly, for example – and being 'inspired'; it's a methodology that's being used by some of the biggest companies and greatest

inventors. Creative thinkers don't think in terms of what they can extract from the natural world, but what they can learn from it. They study nature's best ideas and then imitate them to solve diverse problems.

Nike designers observed mountain goats at Oregon Zoo and developed Goatek Traction, an all-terrain shoe. While travelling in Canada, Clarence Birdseye ate some fish that had been naturally frozen and later thawed. He used nature's idea and the frozen-food industry took off. Dr René Laennac was inspired to invent the stethoscope after seeing a child holding their ear to the end of a long, hollow stick that transmitted and amplified sounds from the opposite end. Turner strapped himself to the mast of a ship in a vicious storm to observe nature and capture its essence in his paintings. Jørn Utzon's iconic design for the Sydney Opera House was inspired by a cut-up orange he had for lunch: the fourteen shells of the building, if assembled together, would form a perfect sphere. George de Mestral, when walking in the country, noticed how burrs stuck to his clothing. By mimicking the small hooks of the burrs he developed Velcro. Japan's Shinkansen bullet train is modelled on the kingfisher's aerodynamic beak. Intertwining ivies that hung in the form of a catenary arch inspired the design of the suspension bridge. Many composers have used birdsong for inspiration: Olivier Messiaen was a particular exponent, and so too were Beethoven, Handel, Mahler and Delius.

Many Silicon Valley companies modelled the way they organise their corporations on living organisms. This enables them to adapt rapidly to changes and restructure themselves quickly in response to market developments.

Whatever your field, nature has produced something that relates to your subject. Explore the animal, vegetable and mineral. What can they teach you? Think of nature not as a source of materials to use but as a library of ideas.

'There is no better designer than nature.'

Alexander McQueen

Keen for natural inspiration but not interested in being practical? *Try p. 31. Curious about transcending natural limits? Consider trying a twenty-six-hour body clock on p. 125.*

don't be an expert on yourself

If you give a lecture or talk about yourself or your work, try to embrace the following attitude: I'm not sure what I do or why; let's work it out together. I once attended a talk by a speaker who spent the first twenty-five minutes telling us how important he was and that he was an expert in his field. It was counterproductive. We all sat there thinking, if you have to tell us how important you are, you're not very important. By chance, soon after that I attended a talk by a famous sculptor who completely disarmed the audience by opening with the assertion that he didn't really understand his work: he tried things out and people seemed to think it was successful so he kept doing it. He asked us, the audience, to explain his work for him. You will only get the most out of your talk if it teaches you about yourself.

☞ Do not take on the role of a schoolteacher and explain everything. Just because it is your work does not mean you are an authority on it.

☞ Do not stand at the front. Stand at the back, walk among the audience or sit in the middle. It breaks things up.

☞ Make the audience stand. If seated, they relax. That's not good. They need to be alert. Standing, you become conscious of their discomfort and keep things short and to the point.

(I once chose to give a lecture from a car park. I drew images on large sheets of paper with a thick pen and shouted up to my audience, who were leaning out of the second-floor windows. They were uncomfortable. I was uncomfortable. That was the point. It forced me to reduce everything to the essentials.)

☞ Randomly select members of the audience to talk about the slides. They always have an unexpected perspective. I once asked the audience to give the talk for me; I learned much more.

☞ The beginning, middle, end format is a killer. Most software has a shuffle option that throws up your images randomly. If no one knows what is coming next – including you – it will be livelier for everyone.

☞ Never read from notes. If you can't remember something, it is not worth saying. And stop speaking before the audience has stopped listening.

☞ If you feel nervous and awkward, comfort yourself with the fact that no one will remember much of your talk anyway, except maybe the images.

I once gave a talk in a lecture theatre full of entrepreneurs and businessmen. My theme was that we are all too easily distracted and need to be more alert and focused. I hired twenty nude male and female models to walk among the audience as I spoke. I assumed the audience would all be distracted. I had underestimated them – they were intelligent, focused individuals and had listened attentively to each word, as I discovered at the question-and-answer session at the end. It didn't matter. The lecture was unforgettable.

If you want to engage an audience it's essential to be engaged yourself. Only give a talk about something you care passionately about. As part of my work at universities I've had to listen to talks on subjects I have no interest in, but if the speaker is passionately interested, I find that I too become absorbed.

'The attraction of the virtuoso for the public is very like that of the circus for the crowd. There is always the hope that something dangerous will happen.'

Claude Debussy

Agree? Rail further against the tyranny of experts on p. 8.
Disagree? See why nudity only really aids public speaking when taken to extremes on p. 209.

be stubborn about compromise

The incredible struggle of Paulo Coelho is an extraordinary example of sheer determination. As a teenager he passionately wanted to become a writer, but his parents considered this madness. They wanted him to become a lawyer, a secure, respectable profession. To 'save' him from his writing ambitions, his parents had him committed to a mental institution three times. He was subjected to electric shock treatment. He refused to compromise. He instinctively knew he was meant to be a writer, and he went on to become an author with a unique vision. His book *The Alchemist* was translated into eighty languages, sold sixty-five million copies worldwide and provided Coelho with unequivocal, lasting financial security.

Creative thinkers appreciate that to compromise and take the sensible and safe route would be a disaster. When Todd McFarlane worked as an illustrator for Marvel Comics, executives told him to tone down his work because it was too gruesome for the Marvel readership. McFarlane quit. He gave up the security of a steady career and started his own company. His hugely successful ventures span publishing, toy production and a film and animation studio. As an artist in business, McFarlane has remained true to his artistic vision no matter what the business cost.

We all come under pressure from our employers, family or friends to compromise, but to make something unique, to do something extraordinary, often requires that you refuse to compromise your ideals. You have no responsibility to live up to others' expectations, but you do have a responsibility to live up to your own expectations.

'Your time is limited; so don't waste it living someone else's life. Don't be trapped by dogma – which is living with the results of other people's thinking. Don't let the noise of others' opinions drown out your own inner voice.'

Steve Jobs

Meet some other writers who refused to give up on p. 241.

be a weapon of mass creation

You owe a great deal to economist Paul Samuelson. In 2008, when the international economy slid into the steepest downturn since the Great Depression, industrialised countries averted disaster by following Samuelson's counter-intuitive advice and raised spending on infrastructure projects, cut taxes, allowed imports to flow in and drove interest rates down to near zero. Contrast this with the Great Depression of the nineteen-thirties, when governments turned a crisis into a disaster by cutting spending, balancing budgets and erecting trade barriers.

When John F. Kennedy was elected in 1960 he appointed Samuelson as his economic adviser, but was shocked by his recommendation. The economy was facing a downturn, and he told Kennedy to cut taxes. It was counter-intuitive and seemed to be the opposite policy to Kennedy's election campaign promise to balance the budget. After Kennedy's assassination his successor, Lyndon B. Johnson, carried out the plan and the economy bounced back. Samuelson remained adviser to subsequent presidents.

Even more shocking was that many of Samuelson's economic theories were inspired by concepts from medicine or physics. For decades he read medical journals in search of ideas that could be transferred to economics, such as Mendelian dynamics. He also applied the equilibrium principles of thermodynamics to economics. He had such a huge impact because he applied creative thinking to economics when everyone else was applying logic.

When he was a student in the nineteen-thirties, Samuelson attended a lecture on economics at the University of Chicago. It was a revelation to him; he realised there and then that he wanted to be an economist. What he brought to the stodgy world of currency graphs, growth estimates and supply-and-demand debates was a creative mind. Discovering his calling made him more alive, more vibrant and more authentic – and this playfulness and inventiveness is what made him so distinguished. He had fun with ideas rather than trying to write Very Serious Papers and be taken Very Seriously. His books were at times so playful they toppled over into inspired childishness. In a footnote to his influential paper, 'Overlapping Generations Model', he wrote, 'Surely, no sentence beginning with the word "surely" can validly contain a question mark at its end? However, one paradox is enough for one article . . .'

Samuelson felt that economics was made for him, and that he was made for it. 'Never underestimate the vital importance of finding early in life the work that for you is play,' he explained. The key to his success was that he introduced ideas from his other interests in physics and science to economics. This turned economics into something personal. He playfully pooled all his interests into economics. 'Always, I have been overpaid to do what has been pure fun,' he said.

Economics was not known for being a creative endeavour; it was a discipline dominated by stale, stuffy and repetitious thinking. Samuelson changed all that. Applying creative thinking in an 'uncreative' field gives you an advantage. An area that's considered 'uncreative', such as admin, accounting, insurance, clinical research, finance, banking, science or any 'serious' industry, is the perfect place to inject creativity, and often the area where creativity is most effective. Creativity is not just for the worlds of art, literature and music.

Like the one-eyed man in the kingdom of the blind, if you think creatively where no one else is, it gives you the edge.

'If you deliberately plan on being less than you are capable of being, then I warn you that you'll be deeply unhappy for the rest of your life. You will be evading your own capacities, your own possibilities.'

Abraham Maslow

Meet a great inventor who found creativity where he least expected on p.183.

get into what you're into

An agency was struggling to come up with ideas for a TV ad and asked for my help. The target audience was the elderly. The ad agency had extensively researched every aspect of the lives of the elderly but it meant little to the two young men working on the ad. They were outside their subject looking in.

I made them BE their subject. I took them both to a theatrical costumier and had them dressed in grey wigs and prosthetic teeth. Their faces were aged with latex moulds and they were given walking sticks and appropriate clothes. They were transformed into authentic-looking eighty-year-olds. The transformation was quite shocking.

I simply asked them to walk about the streets and shops of London. They were astonished by the change in attitude towards them. At best people were patronising; more often they were dismissive or rude. Quite a shock. It was a harrowing experience for them. Suddenly they understood how it felt to be elderly. This experience formed the idea for their ad.

We tend to stand outside what we do, looking in. Detached and analytical. There is a distance between what we are doing and us. To get the most out of life and work, we need to see it from the inside. Whatever you are interested in, get right into it. Imagine you are the subject of your project. If your subject is a cup, try to imagine what it is like to be a cup, to be picked up, to have boiling water poured into you, to smell of coffee, to be put in a dishwasher, to be scratched or chipped. Be the subject from the inside out.

'One had to immerse oneself in one's surroundings and intensely study nature or one's subject to understand how to recreate it.'

Paul Cézanne

Seeking a new perspective? Teach someone a lesson on p. 265.

cut it out

The epic war film *Apocalypse Now* is consistently voted one of the greatest films of all time. Filming started in March 1976 and was scheduled to take six weeks. It took sixteen months. The director, Francis Ford Coppola, shot around 230 hours of footage, with multiple takes of the same scene. He was hoping to capture a magical or unusual performance. He encouraged the actors to ad-lib, which produced some poetic moments but also hours of unusable footage. Once filming was finished, it had to be cut and recut for months. It took Coppola and his film editor Walter Murch nearly three years to edit the footage into the finished *Apocalypse Now*.

Why produce a lot of work and then throw away ninety-five per cent? The two processes seem contradictory. Why not just produce the five per cent ultimately used? Because you don't know *which* five per cent you'll use. Editing can be hard because you're discarding things you have put a lot of energy into making. Yet often what we see of creative thinkers' work is the tip of the iceberg. We don't see the hours, days, weeks and months of hard work and struggle; we just see the end result.

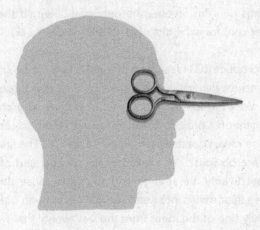

Picasso would have empathised with Coppola. A friend of mine is a specialist picture restorer who conserves paintings by Rembrandt, Titian, Matisse and many other great artists for major museums of the world. For one job, he was flown to Paris twice a year with his team of assistants and taken down into a vast subterranean vault beneath a bank. The armoured, bombproof walls were a metre thick. The two-metre-thick vault doors could only be accessed by an elaborate system of voice recognition and three-foot keys. It required two bank staff to cooperate and open the complex lock simultaneously. Then there were body heat detectors, Doppler radars, magnetic fields and motion detectors. Finally they would emerge into a vast temperature-controlled vault that stretched as far as the eye could see. It was lined on either side by racks containing tens of thousands of unseen Picasso paintings. My friend's task was to inspect them for ageing and make any necessary repairs or restoration. Although Picasso had produced thousands of paintings over his lifetime, he only ever selected the best five per cent for exhibition. He edited out the weak.

If you produce 100 ideas, one of them is likely to be great. If you produce five ideas, the chances of one being great are small. When a company calls me in to work as a creative consultant on a project, instead of getting them to come up with one idea, I get them to come up with 100. The first forty ideas are obvious. The next forty are unusual and offbeat. The last twenty are strange and surreal because they are pushing their minds into areas they've never been before. It is usually one of the ideas from the last twenty that we use. Ninety-nine are cut out. If involved in a task at work, come up with 100 ideas and then pick the best one. It requires more effort, more energy and more discernment, but gives you more choice. You become rich by spending yourself.

'Kill your darlings, kill your darlings, even when it breaks your egocentric little scribbler's heart, kill your darlings.'

Stephen King

Can't bring yourself to cut your creative efforts? *Try reworking them instead, on p. 198.*

grow old without growing up

It takes years to build up the ability to understand yourself, the world you live in and your field of expertise. The architect Zaha Hadid did not achieve international respect for her unique designs and win awards until she was over fifty. Paul Cézanne had his first one-man show at the age of fifty-six. Alfred Hitchcock didn't fully develop his trademark sense of suspense until after he had turned fifty. Jane Austen published her first novel after she was thirty-five. Joseph Conrad's work was first published when he was thirty-seven. Charles Darwin was fifty when he proposed the theory of evolution in *On the Origin of Species* – which sold out on its first day of release.

Artist Georgia O'Keeffe produced remarkable images of the American landscape and still lifes, painted with intimacy and stark precision. She was already in her fifties when she started to gain attention, and throughout her sixties and seventies her fame grew gradually. Her most important exhibition, at the Whitney Museum of American Art, did not come until 1970 when she was in her eighties. It established her as one of America's most significant painters. She didn't grow old in mind because her enthusiasm never waned. At the age of eighty-four, O'Keeffe was rejuvenated by a twenty-six-year-old potter, Juan Hamilton. The two shocked their neighbours in the small town of Abiquiu, New Mexico, with their liaison. They ignored their notoriety, travelled the world together and invigorated each other. They were together until O'Keeffe died at the age of ninety-eight.

Many entrepreneurs, chefs, teachers, writers and artists produce their greatest work as their insights and perceptions deepen with age. Maturity is an advantage when it comes to creativity. The more experience of life you have had the more subject matter there is to draw on. Age brings an understanding of who you are and what your limits are. Creativity is about having something to say.

A creative person can't refuse to grow old but they can refuse to grow up. They maintain the playful attitude of a child throughout their lives. They understand that some things are too serious to take seriously. They never lose the urge to throw a snowball at a businessman. All creativity is about mind over matter. That matter might be paint, ink, paper or almost anything. The matter doesn't matter, because it's all in the mind.

'My breakthrough came very late in life . . . But at that time I felt as though I had the strength for new deeds and ideas.'

Edvard Munch

Inspired? Be mature enough to be childish on p. 89.

if it ain't broke, break it

I'm good friends with the *Venus de Milo*. I see her every week. A cast of her stands in the foyer of Central Saint Martins College of Art, where I teach. My fascination with her never dims. To catch a glimpse of the original *Venus* at the Louvre you have to elbow your way through crowds. Further proof of her enduring popularity is the way she's plastered over mugs, knickers and coasters and reproduced as soap, salt shakers and rubber toys that squeak. She has also inspired artists such as Cézanne, Dalí and Magritte. When the statue was sent to Japan on loan in 1964, one and a half million people were carried past her on a moving sidewalk.

The *Venus de Milo* is full of faults, yet she is the quintessential emblem of classical beauty. The graceful statue of a mysterious, nameless goddess has intrigued and fascinated the world since its discovery in 1820, when it achieved instant fame. It's a classical sculpture that follows an unusually dynamic spiral composition. The *Venus* doesn't exist in our world but in a mysterious and ethereal zone. The delicate flesh has been exquisitely modelled. Serene and remote, her head turns slightly away. With an air of aloofness, her gaze never meets our eyes.

Many ancient statues of Venus exist, but most are too damaged to compete with the *Venus de Milo*, and the remainder are not damaged enough. The statue would have been painted and adorned with jewellery to look lifelike. All traces of original paint have disappeared and the only signs of the armbands, necklace, earrings and crown she used to wear are the attachment holes. Famously, the arms have also been lost. Broken and mutilated she stands; no one knows her original pose. She may have held an apple, a shield or a mirror in which she admired her reflection. We'll never know. It all adds to her intrigue and allure. This is the beauty of imperfection. It is more enlightened to appreciate imperfections; if you search for perfection you will always be disappointed. There is a sense of freedom in accepting its alternative.

The coffee chain Starbucks embraced imperfection. They introduced new concepts quickly. Whether an iced caramel macchiato or a new store design, these concepts were launched before they had been perfected and then improved as they went along. An innovation process that is trying to achieve something faultless is too slow and restricted. Innovation needs errors and failures because they lead to new ideas. The conundrum for organisations is how to foster an innovative culture, with all the messiness and faults that come with it, when the 'perfectionists' in an organisation work to reject imperfection.

Is it ever worthwhile to try to achieve perfection? There are times when we are under pressure to perform flawlessly. Perfectionism can be a roadblock to new ideas; it is a full stop, whereas imperfection can lead somewhere unexpected. High standards are worthwhile, but perfectionism is something else. High standards are about something being as good as it can be. Perfection is about something being free from mistakes and faults.

When my daughter, Scarlet, was at school she had to produce a self-portrait for an art exam. She felt uncomfortable about it, so portrayed herself through frosted glass. It obscured the detail of her features but created a mysterious, blurred and intriguing image. She was worried about what the response would be to a self-portrait that didn't clearly show her face. Her teachers loved it and so too did London's Saatchi Gallery, which later included it in an exhibition.

Strive for imperfection. Miss deadlines, get lost on the way to the airport, forget to reply to emails and show up at parties a day early. It's more interesting. If it's broke, don't fix it; if it ain't broke, break it.

'The essence of being human is that one does not seek perfection.'

George Orwell

Agree? *Plan to have more accidents on p. 110.*
Disagree? *Discover the merits of perseverance and perfectionism through one of history's great inventors in the next chapter.*

pick yourself up

I meet a great many talented artists, writers and musicians in my work as a lecturer, both at Central Saint Martins and in the art world. Many go on to be successful but many others don't. What distinguishes the successful from the unsuccessful is the way they deal with the inevitable disappointments and difficulties that arise. Psychologists call it the 90–10 principle. Ten per cent of life is what happens to you and ninety per cent is decided by how you react to what happens to you. We have no control over ten per cent of what happens to us – high winds rip the roof off, your train is delayed or a meteorite lands on your car. The ninety per cent is different. You determine it.

James Dyson is a remarkable example of this positive trait. After he came up with the idea for the world's first cyclone vacuum cleaner he worked for the next five years, designing, making and testing more than 5,000 prototypes. That means 4,999 failures that he had to pick himself up from. Quite a feat. He also had to finance it all himself.

When Dyson finally produced a satisfactory model, he tried to sell it to manufacturers of traditional bag-type vacuum cleaners but they all rejected his bagless device. Eventually he sold his idea to a company in Japan, where it became a commercial success and won a design prize. Dyson opened a plant and within two years his Dual Cyclone model became the top-selling vacuum cleaner in Britain and spread across the world. Dyson's elegant and practical appliances have gone on to win many design awards and be exhibited in art and design museums around the world.

The key difference in successful creative people is their reaction to negative events. You can't control a meteorite landing on your car but you can control your reaction to it. When things go wrong, it triggers frustration, anger and disappointment in everyone. Some people fall into a downward spiral of negativity and abandon their project. The creative thinker is able to put aside their annoyance and adopt a positive attitude – and therefore achieve a positive result. I was waiting for a train with my son Louis once when the station loudspeakers announced that it had been delayed by an hour. The other passengers started moaning and angrily shouted at the railway staff. For them the next hour was dead time. For Louis it was an opportunity. He took out his sketchpad and started sketching the angry passengers. He was disappointed when the train arrived. His reaction was a reminder to me that there is no 'dead time': we should always be doing something like writing, drawing or just thinking.

What we learn from creative thinkers is that they control their negative feelings and channel them into something useful. Everyone is irritable and disappointed when things go wrong, but the creative quickly rally and try again. Their desire to produce something excellent overrides momentary failure. Attitude is more important than ability.

'The people who are crazy enough to think they can change the world, are the ones who do.'

Apple's 1997 'Think Different' commercial

Meet Ted Turner, the entrepreneur who truly made things happen, on p. 227.

challenge the challenging

When the great inventor Thomas Edison hired bright young engineer Nikola Tesla to work in his New York office in 1884, he took on more than he had bargained for. Tesla was recommended because he was considered to be a genius comparable to Edison. Tesla designed several products for Edison, but didn't receive his promised bonus ($1 million in today's money), so he stormed out.

Edison's use of direct current (DC) to carry electricity to consumers was a monopoly. Tesla invented a new method using alternating current (AC). Unlike DC it could transmit huge amounts of power over long distances. Edison condemned Tesla's AC as dangerous because of its high voltage and demonstrated this by publicly electrocuting an elephant in New York in August 1890. The botched and horrific killing needed two attempts. It didn't stop an investor from backing Tesla's AC technology and eventually Tesla won through. The bitter rivalry bore fruit.

Having a rival can be useful, as they drive us to the limits of our ability. Thomas Edison went head to head with Nikola Tesla, Bill Gates with Steve Jobs, and for Constable there was Turner. They all benefitted from their rivalry, pushing each other to greater things. In hard times when they struggled for motivation, they were spurred on by the achievements of the other. Competition can help everyone reach greater heights. It creates intensity and passion and makes you work harder and better. If there is someone in your office, factory or workplace who constantly tries to outdo you, rise to the challenge.

During the nineteen-twenties, brothers Adolf and Rudolf created the Dassler Brothers Sports Shoe Company, a business based in their mother's laundry room in Herzogenaurach, Germany. By 1948 they had split into two separate firms, with competing factories on opposite sides of town. Their mutual determination to produce the better trainer led them to be world leaders in their field: Adolf's company was Adidas, Rudolf's was Puma. Herzogenaurach became known as 'the town of bent necks' because residents were constantly checking to see which of the two brands their neighbours were wearing.

Like the Dasslers, it helps if your rival is roughly at the same level, not a great deal lower or higher, because you have a realistic chance of outdoing them. In 2012 Apple was declared the biggest company in the world. Steve Jobs hadn't set out to overtake the biggest companies of the time, Coke or Nike, though; his rivalry was with Bill Gates.

They were both the same age, started their businesses at the same time and in similarly humble circumstances and were on an equal level. The fruits of their rivalry were Microsoft's Windows, which became the world's default operating system, and Apple's iPhone, iPad and iPod. 'And every fantasy we had about creating products and learning new things – we achieved all of it. And most of it as rivals,' said Bill Gates. In 1997 Apple was facing financial doom. Their unlikely saviour? Microsoft, who stepped in to save them by investing $150 million in Apple shares. Why did Gates bail out Apple? Perhaps Gates sensed that he needed Jobs' rivalry. They had a mutual respect and became friendly in the years before Jobs died. Having fought each other for so long, they knew better than anyone what the other had accomplished.

Although rivalry can energise and motivate creative people, it's important that it doesn't divert you away from your own strengths and your own path. Jobs remained faithful to his design strengths and Gates was true to his technical strengths. The rivalry between the English painters Constable and Turner pushed them both to achieve the best they could in the same field, but with contrasting approaches. The two painters were different characters. Constable was refined and conventional, Turner immoral and vulgar. Constable was diffident and sensitive, Turner assertive and friendly. Turner was short and instinctive, Constable tall and reflective. Which is the greater artist is debatable but both reached the summit of their achievements by trying to outdo each other.

A famous example of their rivalry was when they displayed paintings side by side at the Royal Academy in 1832. John Constable exhibited a colourful painting that had taken him fifteen years to paint next to a grey seascape by Turner that had taken him a few hours. The day before the exhibition opened, varnishing day, artists were allowed to add finishing touches to their work. Turner noticed that his serene seascape looked lacklustre in comparison to Constable's. He took out his paints and added a small red daub in the water, a buoy, and then left without saying a word. Turner's quick, deft stroke made the painting complete. Constable's painting then looked overworked in comparison. It was Turner's way of saying 'Less is more'. Constable was in another gallery when the retouching happened, and when he returned to see it he gasped, 'Turner has been here and fired a gun.' From then on Constable got his retaliation in first; he often put a small figure in a red jacket in the foreground of his landscapes.

Psychology tells us that rivalry has the potential to both help and hinder creative success – it all depends on how we handle the competition. The benefits of competitiveness were demonstrated by psychologists in a study led by Tim Rees at the University of Exeter. They recruited students to carry out a darts challenge while blindfolded, and a researcher dressed as a supporter of a rival university tried to demoralise the students by criticising their performance. The students' later performances were better because they were motivated to prove their rival wrong.

Whatever your field, embrace competition: it can make you strive to be better, to go that extra mile. Chances are, you too have at least one close rival. Monitor their achievements with admiration, and a touch of envy.

'I'm not going to get into the ring with Tolstoy.'

Ernest Hemingway

Feeling collaborative rather than competitive? *Meet the scientist without whom you probably wouldn't be alive on p. 246.*

find out how to find out

I vividly remember walking along Fifth Avenue in New York on my first trip there, passing block after block of rectangular, ornamented apartment houses, oppressive in their uniformity, monotonous in their regularity. Then the gleaming white Solomon R. Guggenheim Museum burst into view, a breathtaking symphony of ovals, arcs and circles.

This museum doesn't look like any building you've ever seen before. That's because the architect Frank Lloyd Wright was self-taught. He had to work out for himself how to design a building. Wright found his own way. Ignorance of the 'right' way to do something can be an asset; if you do things the way they've been taught, your methods will be the same as everyone else's and you'll produce something obvious, predictable. The regular buildings were designed by architects taught the regular way. If you make up your own method, it's likely to be a *new* method, one that produces new results. Lack of knowledge can provide fresh perspectives.

The Guggenheim is as impressive inside as out. A spiral ramp rises up through the building to a domed skylight. It is a unique concept that delights visitors and provides an original way of displaying contemporary art. The circle is the form that echoes through the building from the rotunda to the terrazzo floors. By discarding the static box shapes of conventional museums and replacing them with the flexibility of this building, Wright produced a building that's as refreshing now as it was in 1959 when it opened. Every major museum is indebted to the Guggenheim; it has made it acceptable for an architect to design an expressive, intensely personal museum.

Frank Lloyd Wright attended Madison High School, but didn't graduate. He was admitted to university but left without taking a degree. He was hired as a draughtsman for an architectural firm and taught himself about architecture. He designed many houses with the radical approach of using mass-produced materials developed for commercial buildings. Wright rejected the elaborate compartmentalisation of the time and created bold, plain walls, roomy family living spaces and large glazed areas. His technical deficiencies meant that he often overlooked mundane practicalities and so his roofs leaked, he ignored budgets and his buildings were beset by a host of technical problems; but his clients appreciated that they were getting a design classic.

Wright consistently broke the rules. Not to be rebellious – he simply hadn't been taught them. He produced work that felt right to him. Sometimes, knowing the 'right way' can be a disadvantage.

John Harrison was not held back by the 'right way'. In 1730 he invented the marine chronometer, a clock with a unique mechanism that enabled it to remain accurate even on a ship in a storm. This solved the problem of determining longitude at sea accurately, which had cost the lives of countless sailors for centuries.

Harrison was completely self-taught and had no training in clock-making. His biography notes: '. . . if Harrison had served an apprenticeship in the usual way, learning from a master, he might not have imagined [such a clock] either; he would have learned whatever the master had to teach, he would have done what he was taught and done it well, and made a very good living at it – without risk, without the danger of failure.'

The alternative to training is not no training, but instead to equip students with the thought processes that enable them to think for themselves. Our culture needs more untrained minds. Seemingly a strange position to be in if, like me, you teach at a university. You encourage students not to listen to you but to themselves, to have the confidence to think unconventionally.

Schools and universities teach tried-and-tested techniques. Schools follow the banking model of learning and see knowledge as a currency to be stacked up and locked away. Students enter schools as question marks and leave as full stops. Everyone is born with more abilities than they realise. Most are born geniuses and are de-geniused by education and convention.

We don't learn to walk by reading a book on how to walk. We learn by walking, falling over, getting up and trying again. There is no right way of doing anything. So you must find your way. Wherever you work, try to work out for yourself how to do things.

'If I'd observed all the rules, I'd never have got anywhere.'

Marilyn Monroe

Discover the joys of doubting everyone and everything on p. 40.

Discover the joys of doubting everyone and everything on p. 40.

leave an impression

The names of ex-students killed in World War Two were carved on a plaque at Yale University. A sculpture student, Maya Lin, couldn't resist running her fingers over them whenever she passed by. Touching the grooves of the names gave her a sense of deep connection with the fallen soldiers. It was something she never forgot.

Lin remembered that sensation when designing the ground-breaking Vietnam Veterans Memorial in Washington, DC, a long, black stone wall with the names of all fallen soldiers carved on it. There are no ranks or details; everyone is equal. There are nearly sixty thousand names and most died very young. The stone was chosen for its reflective quality; when a visitor looks at the wall, their reflection can be seen simul-taneously with the engraved names, which symbolically brings the past and present together. Most memorials are remote and untouchable bronze sculptures of soldiers, but over the decades millions of visitors have run their fingers across the carved names of the Vietnam memorial. Lin simply replicated what had inspired her about the plaque at

Yale University but on a larger scale. Even if you don't know anyone who died in Vietnam, it's heart-wrenching to watch the poignant sight of visitors earnestly studying the names to find their loved ones, or rubbing pencil on paper held against a name etched into the wall.

Drawing attention to something that amazes, excites or stimulates is often enough. Make the most of what you have seen or experienced. If it fascinates you, it is likely to fascinate others. Creativity can be as simple as pointing out something incredible that everyone else hasn't noticed. Note down anything that astounds you, no matter how small. You never know when you might be able to use it. If it left an impression on you, it will leave an impression on others.

'Art is not what you see, but what you make others see.'

Edgar Degas

Inspired? *Join Truman Capote in refusing to overlook the overlooked on p. 131.*

Uninspired? *Forget about making an impression on others and meet the most successful class in history, in which every student won a Nobel Prize, on p. 35.*

design a difference

A package arrived and I tore it open expectantly. Inside was something unexpected. A sleek, fourteen-inch, egg-shaped object. The white-and-Bondi Blue-coloured shell was translucent like polished ice but tougher than bulletproof glass. The colour combination was new and oddly alien. Its vitreous nature allowed me a blurry glimpse of the innards. The smoothness, absence of joins or grooves and magical weightlessness made it feel as though it could not have been created in a factory but only by alchemy. It seemed like an object from another universe, a visual wonder that you needed to run your hands over to believe it was real. It was otherworldly, created by an alien culture far more technologically advanced than any previously encountered.

I had been sent the new iMac G3. Back in the late nine-teen-nineties, it seemed unearthly. Like a lot of other people, I began to wonder what magician had created it and what supernatural powers he'd used.

Steve Jobs used his small amount of knowledge about design to make a big difference. Apple products became famous for style. While their competitors concentrated on the technical aspects of computers, Jobs focused on aesthetics. Until the iMac, computers had been ugly and uncool. What made him think so differently?

Jobs only attended the classes he liked at college, ones that interested him. He saw a beautifully designed poster advertising a calligraphy class. It was so appealing he felt compelled to attend. He learned that each typeface has its own unique personality. There is as much meaning conveyed by the design of the typeface as the words. Typography was functional, but could also be seductive. He found it artistically subtle in a way science couldn't capture.

Jobs positioned Apple at the intersection of art and computing; he united technology and design, and introduced elegance and style to a product that up until then had been geeky and clumsy. Because he attended that calligraphy course, the Mac had numerous typefaces, aesthetically spaced fonts and an emphasis on design. This gave Apple the edge over its rivals. Windows copied Jobs' values; in this way, all personal computers were influenced. Apple was not a technological innovator; it remade other companies' ideas. IBM introduced the personal computer first; Nokia invented the smartphone first. When Apple tried innovation it was hopeless. Remember the Newton? The Power Mac G4 Cube? Neither does anyone else. 'We did tablets, lots of tablets, well before Apple did. But they put the pieces together in a way that succeeded,' recalled Bill Gates. As

Jobs recalled, 'For you to sleep well at night, the aesthetic, the quality, has to be carried all the way through.'

Entrepreneurs and creative thinkers make the most of whatever information they have, however little. They constantly sift through all the facts they've picked up and put even the smallest piece to good use. Armed with a small amount of knowledge, Jobs fought against the conventional thinking of the computer industry and won. Jobs demonstrated that to create good design you often need as little design as possible. A small nugget of knowledge that you've overlooked could be the key that unlocks doors that have previously been closed to you.

'A designer knows he has achieved perfection not when there is nothing left to add, but when there is nothing left to take away.'

Antoine de Saint-Exupéry

Meet the world's best designed – and least functional – kitchen implement on p. 31.

be as incompetent as possible

I sat and watched a clock for twenty-four hours, completely enthralled.

Artist Christian Marclay's film installation *The Clock* is made of a twenty-four-hour montage of thousands of time-related scenes from movies, edited and shown in 'real time'. Each clip contains the time on a clock or watch or in a clip of dialogue when people refer to the time. There are shots of sundials from black and white movies, a clip from *Easy Rider* where Peter Fonda looks at his watch (showing 11:40 a.m.), then throws it away, and the 'Alas, poor Yorick!' scene from Olivier's *Hamlet* when a distant bell tolls the quarter-hour. *The Clock* is synchronised so that whatever time is shown is the correct time in the 'real world'. The film is a gigantic and completely impractical clock. The viewer is encouraged to think about the nature of time in the cinema and in life. *The Clock* is a masterpiece that will run and run, without ever needing to be wound, because it's powered by a strong idea. Marclay has little technical skill to marvel at; it's his concepts that are hugely impressive. Our minds remember powerful ideas long after they have forgotten impressive skill.

Creative thinking is about vision, awareness and expression. Skill is useful, but not essential. It's important to avoid the trap of wanting to impress people with skill, and it's easy to confuse this with ability. Ability is about your innate sensibility and understanding. Skill is about training and repetition. Is the great opera singer who forces him or herself to practise for hours each day expressing a love of music, or merely exploiting a skill? Enjoying music for the sake of it is rewarding. The creative mind explores whatever it is fascinated by rather than building up an armoury of skills.

Running a large and successful business requires a high level of skill to deal with balance sheets, business management, finance and accounting. Or does it? Sir Richard Branson is an English business magnate, best known as the founder of the multimillion-pound Virgin Group, which consists of more than four hundred companies. His poor maths skills were once exposed in a board meeting when Virgin's director realised that Branson didn't understand the difference between net and gross profit. The director drew a sea, then fishes in a net (profit) and some fishes outside (turnover). Branson understood the maths when it had been transformed into a visual image. He was surprised and disappointed – he'd thought it was the other way round – and realised Virgin wasn't making as much money as he'd thought. Knowing the difference between net and gross is an elementary business skill, yet without it he had created an empire with 60,000 employees. Branson's lack of maths skills was an advantage – because he didn't get caught up in financial details he could see the big picture. He had other people to do the maths. Branson may have no business skill but he does have an ability for business – a gut instinct for what the public want and how to deliver it.

A lack of skill and expertise prevented a student in one of my workshops from fulfilling their lifetime dream of opening a restaurant. We came up with the idea of a takeaway restaurant, a restaurant without a kitchen where customers could order from the menus of nearby takeaways and have their food delivered to their table. A waiter advised them on the quality and estimated delivery time of the different meals, placed the order, received the order, removed the packaging, put the food on a plate and served it. My student had no restaurant experience or skills but in this way was able to open a restaurant. Eventually he and his colleagues had built up enough resources to hire a chef and kitchen equipment and slowly began to serve their own recipes.

When someone emphasises technique rather than the concept, it is proof that they have run out of ideas. The genuinely creative are not seeking to display skill but have a sincere interest in understanding and expressing ideas about their subject. Those with mechanical minds seek perfect technique by asking 'How?'. But those with curiosity seek understanding by asking 'Why?'

'Sometimes incompetence is useful. It helps you keep an open mind.'

Roberto Cavalli

More? Be a beginner forever on p. 8.

be mature enough to be childish

Steve Jobs was astonished. As CEO of Apple he'd given young start-up design group Hovey-Kelley their big break, a commission that could have established their reputation. Apple had a global reputation for elegant design, yet they presented him with something that looked like it had been produced by a bunch of five-year-olds in playschool. Assorted scraps, a ball from a roll-on deodorant, a piece of a refrigerator, bits of a car gearstick and a dish from a super-market, all held together with tape and rubber bands.

David Kelley and his colleagues were grown men with a business to run and they'd spent days playing like children. They played around with scraps of objects and playschool materials. They'd had a lot of fun, but then they had to present the result to Jobs with his notoriously high standards.

In the early nineteen-eighties products were formally designed in detailed drawings and then fabricated to these specifications. It was a lengthy and sophisticated process. Very grown up, very serious. Kelley didn't want to work that way. It was too slow and restrictive. He wanted to play around with whatever materials were to hand and make a prototype fast. It was a crude creation but it visualised an idea quickly.

Jobs instantly understood what this mishmash of bits and pieces meant. It was a revolutionary new computer mouse, one of the most sophisticated yet accessible pieces of technology ever made. Previous versions of the mouse could only be moved in a linear up, down and across motion, were full of fussy little parts and were very expensive to make. The basic principle in Kelley's prototype, pairing a freely rolling ball (the roll-on deodorant) with an optoelec-tronic system, was used by generations of mice. Billions were made. Due to its success, Hovey-Kelley blossomed into IDEO, the renowned international design consultancy.

How do you get adults to take play seriously? When giving a lecture, I've often tried an experiment made famous by Bob McKim, an eminent researcher into creativity in the nineteen-seventies (he was a big influence on IDEO). I give everyone a pen and paper and ask them to draw the person next to them, then show each other their drawings. The reaction is always embarrassed laughter and repeated apologies.

McKim felt this proved how much we fear others' judge-ment. We're embarrassed about showing our ideas and this apprehension makes us unadventurous. Contrast this with the reaction of children undertaking the same exercise. They demonstrate a complete lack of inhibition. They're confident to show their work to anyone. Studies show that when children are in a secure environment they feel most free to play. The same is true of adults.

My main role as a tutor at university and as a creative consultant is to set up a situation where people feel confident enough to be playful. Being playful is what enables us to develop. When organisations tell me they aren't generating enough ideas and are falling behind their competitors, it's usually because their people are fearful and insecure. Scared of what their boss or colleagues will think; scared they'll get it 'wrong'.

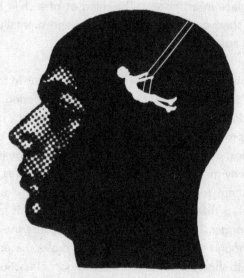

Artists like Jean Dubuffet in the nineteen-forties led the way in reappraising the value of play. He was fascinated by the sense of freedom expressed in children's art. It was generally dismissed as worthless and primitive, but Dubuffet saw it as fresh and unselfconscious. He didn't simply copy the style of children's art; he copied their raw, innocent approach. He realised that although there were many benefits to maturity, he had forgotten one essential ingredient of creativity: play.

Dubuffet resolved to return to the unfettered mindset of childhood when he was working. His paintings became full of the life, savage energy and inventiveness of the child. He worked with the unprejudiced joy of an infant trying out everything, fascinated by everything. Despite his work receiving the 'a child of five could do that' jibes from critics, Dubuffet eventually gained an international reputation and a place in art history. The mindset of a child helped him to stay young, both emotionally and mentally, even into old age.

A firm plagued by executive burnout called me in to see if I could prevent their best managers from suffering mental exhaustion. Stress leave was costing the company millions in lost productivity. The executives told me that packed schedules, deadlines and responsibility meant the job was no fun any more. I asked them to list fun activities, then I asked them to list how long they took. The executives discovered that most of their enjoyable activities took a day or longer. They weren't having fun because they didn't have enough time to fit them in. We broke the activities down into short mini-breaks of half an hour or less. Suddenly there were outlets for fun at many points during the day. Stress levels plummeted, production soared and, more importantly, they felt more fulfilled in both their working and private lives.

Blame society, parents, culture, schools or whoever, but generally speaking our freedom to be childlike is buried, and instead inhibition flourishes. We become afraid of being wrong, judged or laughed at. Our fear of creating holds us back and prevents us trying new methods for the sheer joy of it.

The future belongs to those who can reconnect with play. It is the child in you that is creative, not the adult. The child is free and does not know what they can't or shouldn't do. They haven't found what works, whereas adults repeat whatever worked last time. Whatever you are doing, do it as if for the first time. To children there is no last time. Every time is the first time. They explore a land without rules or preconceptions. Somewhere between childhood and adulthood this ability is stifled. Schools teach you something – then test you. In life you are tested – and it teaches you something. The latter is the only effective way to learn.

'There are children playing in the streets who could solve some of my top problems in physics, because they have modes of sensory perception that I lost long ago.'

Robert Oppenheimer

Still need cheering up? Stay playful on p. 250.

maintain momentum

When F. Scott Fitzgerald had an idea for a story he completely devoted himself to developing it. One of the greatest writers of the twentieth century, he wrote the classic novel *The Great Gatsby*, which defined the nineteen-twenties 'Jazz Age' (a term he coined himself).

Fitzgerald wrote and rewrote his stories repeatedly. He lived and breathed the tale and worked on the narrative every day without a break until it was finished, relentlessly rereading and editing his own writing over and over again, day after day. He explained this as stubbornness. As a result, complex sentences gallop like wild horses in all directions, but always with Fitzgerald's firm hand on the reins. The reader senses he writes when on fire, in the zone. Writing and rewriting the stories intensified his unique voice. He wrote in a way that was uniquely his own. He honed each sentence to perfection.

A great idea is electrifying and exhilarating. It has energy. But no matter how strong the idea, if you sit on it it gets cold. You must maintain the sense of excitement you had when first inspired. Whatever the project – building a house extension, renovating a boat or planning to open a store – it's important to maintain the momentum. Work on an idea constantly until it's resolved. The minute we lose momentum, we lose the thread. Our inner critic awakens. We start doubting what we're doing and energy levels drop. When it comes to creative execution, the key is to get moving – and keep moving.

'From the beginning of Queen there was such momentum that I never had any time to do anything else. My energy was ninety-five per cent focused on the band.'

Brian May

Meet one writer who wouldn't give up on p. 53, and another who had no idea where he would end up in the next chapter.

aspire to have no goals

Cut up this page with a pair of scissors. Slice up some words and sentences. Shuffle them and then rearrange them in a way that completely changes the original meaning. You will find that extraordinary things happen; unpredictable and unusual phrases will fall into place. You are freed from the usual structures and purposes of writing and are led in all sorts of mind-expanding directions.

A goal defines the outcome. When you have a goal, the route to it becomes a labour. The imagination becomes closed to other possibilities. If the process is interesting, the result will be interesting. The creative explore in a truly open and experimental way; they don't start with a destination in mind, because a target would trap them on a predetermined path. The search for an objective becomes a barrier to real creativity and exploration. Go out looking for one thing, and that's all you'll ever find. A moth has a goal, the flame, but it is burned up by it.

The writer who best exemplifies this is William Burroughs. He became one of the most influential authors of modern culture because he didn't set out with a clear goal in mind when starting a novel. He used a cut-up technique to create an alternative to traditional, linear narratives. When he started a novel, he had no idea what it would be about or who the characters would be. Sentences from a news-paper, book or other piece of writing were sliced up and then pasted back together, often at random. Burroughs' process constantly threw up unusual combinations and surprising phrases, which kept him excited and engaged in his writing. Unexpected pathways opened up to him. Burroughs freed himself from the conventions and representational straitjacket of the linear novel with a beginning, middle and end, and in doing so became a literary phenomenon.

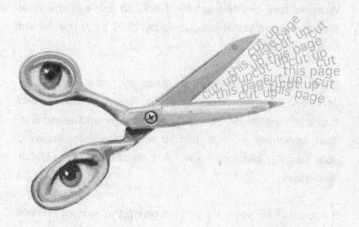

A goal limits your actions. There isn't room to explore other pathways. You have to follow the plan, even when some-thing more exciting emerges. We're taught to make goals that are precise and have time limitation, but this is the exact reason why goals backfire – they encourage us to focus narrowly. The advantages of setting goals are often exaggerated and the downside ignored. A 2009 Harvard Business School paper titled 'Goals Gone Wild: The Systematic Side Effects of Over-Prescribing Goal Setting' came to a similar conclusion. Its authors identified the clear side effects associated with goal-setting, including 'a narrow focus'. Among the case studies they cite is Sears's strategy of setting a goal for their auto repair staff to bring in $147 for every hour of work. It motivated their employees – but it motivated them to overcharge, which damages the reputation of a company. Another example was the case of the Ford Pinto that ignited when it was rear-ended and resulted in fifty-three deaths and many injuries. Workers had omitted safety checks to achieve the goal they had been set of producing by 1970 a car that would cost under $2,000.

Don't want your opponent to guess your strategy? Follow John von Neumann's advice in his *Theory of Games and Economic Behavior*: cut up your strategy and remake it. Your opponent will not gain an advantage from knowing your strategy because he will not be able to predict your next move.

If you don't know where you are going the journey is more surprising and your work is more enriching. The highest purpose is to have no purpose at all. The drive towards achievements is important, but rather than identifying goals it is better to identify areas of focus. A goal defines an outcome but an area of focus establishes what to spend time on. A goal is a result; an area of focus is a gateway. Don't plan how to work, just work.

'You are lost the instant you know what the result will be.'

Juan Gris

Find out more about how doing nothing can achieve great things on p. 173.

make the present a present

Our ability to immerse ourselves in the present, and to live in the moment, is one we must nurture. The composer Maurice Ravel realised this during his extraordinary experiences in World War One. Deployed as a truck driver, Ravel was never safe from the relentless artillery shells, enemy snipers, poison gas and machine-gun fire as he zigzagged along cratered roads supplying the front lines. In winter, the ground froze hard. In spring, rain turned the battlefields to mud. Soldiers' feet swelled to three times their normal size in the water, which often turned them gangrenous and resulted in amputation. Rats grew to the size of dogs by feeding off the rotting corpses littering no-man's-land. The stench of open latrines and rotting bodies was inescapable. Ravel suffered exposure, frostbite and dysentery. The deafening noise made his ears ring even during the rare moments of silence.

Early one sunny morning, Ravel was driving down roads lined with dead, blasted trees, through bleak, bombed-out towns. The light was crisp and clear and in the distance he saw a wrecked château. Inside he miraculously discovered an Érard piano in perfect condition. He sat and played some Chopin and the surrounding horror melted away. He created an ecstatic, exhilarating moment for himself. He became fully involved in the music and immersed himself in the present, later describing it as one of the highlights of his life. Perhaps the surrounding horror made the pleasure that much more intense.

How was Ravel able to shut out the surrounding war? Reading Ravel's letters and accounts of him by his friends reveals that he understood his thinking and moods. He controlled his own thoughts and feelings rather than letting them control him. Many people believe that their thoughts are something that happens to them, instead of something they are making happen. Ravel, though, understood the workings of his mind and the fact that he was manufacturing his own moods. He could create an emotional distance from his surroundings and focus on the here and now. He didn't allow past regrets and future concerns to ruin the present. If you believe your thinking is caused by outside people and events, it's overwhelming. You feel helpless. Ravel could control his attitude to events. An important factor was his interest in music; all artists speak of how they lose themselves in their art, how the outside world melts away and they are totally focused on the task. Ravel was used to this process and knew how to use it. That's why it's important to find tasks that totally engage you.

Ravel wrote some of his most popular works, such as Le tombeau de Couperin, in the midst of war. He turned his traumatic surroundings and experiences into something positive. Ravel believed that the purpose of life was to taste experience, whether good or bad, and reach out for newer and richer ones. Pleasure is not over there but here. Not in the future, but now.

It's important to adore what you do, and become totally immersed in it. The psychologist Mihaly Csikszentmihalyi explains, 'Flow is being completely involved in an activity for its own sake. The ego falls away. Time flies. Every action, movement, and thought follows inevitably from the previous one, like playing jazz.'

Wherever you are and whatever you do, become totally engrossed. You must be utterly into whatever you're experiencing, whether beautiful or ugly, good or bad. Your present circumstances don't dictate your destination, they only determine your departure point.

'Real generosity towards the future lies in giving all to the present.'

Albert Camus

Yes? *Seize the moment and maintain momentum on p. 94.*
No? *Take a year off to get back on track on p. 107.*

open your mind

Andy Warhol's open mind was reflected in the way his studio operated. The door was always open. Anyone could walk in off the street and talk to him, make suggestions or even help make the artworks. There was no privacy. No individual working areas. Everything was open for everyone to see.

A large group of creative individuals slowly formed in his studio, drawn by this attitude of openness. They helped with Warhol's work, suggesting ideas for paintings and even producing them. Warhol was like a sponge; he soaked up the ideas that were flying around in the studio. His followers were a sounding board – different people with diverse but complementary talents and remarkable personalities, who were given the freedom of the studio. Warhol didn't exercise authority. Stimulated by their many talents, he gave them a free hand. He was passive, a void towards which others gravitated with ideas. It was an exciting creative atmosphere where people felt free to contribute ideas. Many felt for the first time in their lives the freedom to truly be themselves. The studio became a hub for all kinds of experimental art, including music. The legendary rock band the Velvet Underground and Lou Reed were protégés of Warhol. The studio had a flat structure – there was no hierarchy. Warhol made everyone feel that they could take part, that everyone had something to offer, and in turn this helped Warhol to feel the pulse of the contemporary world and react like a seismograph to new developments and trends. His assistants felt confident in suggesting radical new ideas because they knew he'd be grateful.

The benefits of the way Warhol's studio operated were so clear that they have been copied extensively in the art world. Jeff Koons, Anselm Kiefer, Damien Hirst and others have all adopted his operating methods. And, although Warhol's studio may seem as if it was only possible in the art world, its influence has in fact permeated much deeper; his system also filtered through to design companies and to more traditional businesses.

Many of the companies that function most successfully have adopted a flat structure. Usually in flat companies everyone owns a chunk of the company, which makes them genuinely committed to the cause. They have few or no levels of middle management between staff and executives. Workers are more productive when directly involved in decision-making, rather than being closely supervised by middle management. Employees feel more responsible. Comments and feedback reach people quickly. With a flat structure, the workforce can decide jointly on the right team for whatever task arises. It also eliminates the fear of being judged by your boss; a boss is always afraid of what their boss thinks, and so on. Fear is duplicated, quadrupled and multiplied. Middle management stop inspiring creative thinkers and instead spread paralysis through their anxieties.

Creativity thrives in a workplace or studio that is open to possibilities and new ideas, no matter how crazy they might appear, knowing they will not be laughed at but taken seriously. An open studio creates open minds. To an open mind there are multiple solutions. A fixed mind only has one possible solution, and cannot cope with change. It is rigid. It snaps when flexed.

'The barriers are not erected which can say to aspiring talents and industry, "Thus far and no farther."'

Ludwig van Beethoven

More? Discover why janitors love working at Pixar on p. 175, and why Bill Gates doesn't mind the right thing being in the wrong place on p. 133.

pause for thoughtlessness

There is an art to doing nothing, intensely. The geniuses of the twenty-first century will be those who can unplug from the unyielding flow of incoming communication: emails, texts, tweets, Facebook, phone calls, and on and on. There's no hiding place from screens; we work at them, they entertain us, there are screens by escalators, in schools and in our pockets to fill the gaps when we are not looking at permanent screens. Genius is so rare today because we are so distracted, updated and connected. Rather than steering life we're reacting to whatever pours in. To work intensively for long periods you need to switch off occasionally for short periods.

Degas, Monet and other Impressionist painters often worked intensively with strong colours in strong sunlight from dawn to dusk. They developed a technique of taking a five-minute break by looking into 'black mirrors' made from the stone obsidian. This soothed their eyes and gave their conscious minds a break. They found that although they were not consciously thinking about the work, the machinery of their minds continued whirring. They returned to work refreshed and energised. They discovered that their eyes saw more and their fingers felt more. Everything seemed richer. They were totally in the moment. No memories pulled them backwards and no plans pulled them forward. The answers to the problems they had been struggling with would suddenly become clear to them.

Working 24/7 is the Western way. We're all ambitious and want to succeed. It feels wrong to stop, even for a moment. It's counter-intuitive, but shutting a business down for a year may be the best way for it to grow. Every seven years designer Stefan Sagmeister shuts down his studio for twelve months. 'Everything that we designed in the seven years following the first sabbatical had its roots in thinking done during that sabbatical,' he has said. Simon Cohen, the founder of Global Tolerance, also made the counter-intuitive choice to place his entire communications agency on a one-year sabbatical. Global Tolerance had grown rapidly, gained high-profile clients and was highly successful. Cohen decided the company needed a rest and time to reflect, which was only going to be possible by taking a year out. Logistically, it wasn't easy. 'Our HR people said there was no such thing as a company sabbatical. It had never been done before,' he said. They made arrangements to prevent their clients from being stolen by competitors and after a year they came back stronger and better.

If you're a manager, allow employees to take a day or a week out. If you're a corporate leader, use a sabbatical system to refresh your workers. If you work for yourself, force yourself to do nothing occasionally. We tend not to rate shutting down but it's more than just an absence of work; it's a tool for recovery. It's important to completely clear your mind. Only when you achieve this can you begin again, refreshed. To think deeply, sometimes you first have to empty your mind of all thoughts.

'Now and then it's good to pause in our pursuit of happiness and just be happy.'

Guillaume Apollinaire

Still not convinced? Mine your mind for your breakthrough idea on p. 183.

plan to have more accidents

You spill a cup of coffee over your work; your pen leaks, or the printer goes crazy. It happens to everyone. Don't automatically discard accidents but instead work with them. Go along with them and see where they lead. Use them to propel yourself forward in unexpected directions.

The problem is not the accident; the problem is you. Override your preprogrammed and preconceived ideas that accidents are something going wrong. You need to be more receptive to the unexpected. The painter Francis Bacon summed up the creative person's attitude to chance: 'All painting is an accident. But it's also not an accident, because one must select what part of the accident one chooses to preserve.'

In everyday life everyone tries to avoid accidents in their work. Far from being annoyed by accidents, however, creative people are intrigued by them. The most successful scientists have not thought like scientists – in a logical, linear way – but more like artists. If something goes 'wrong', they look for the 'right' in it.

Édouard Bénédictus accidentally knocked a glass beaker from a shelf. The beaker broke. Surprisingly and shockingly, it didn't shatter into small shards but broke into a few large pieces. As well as being a composer, writer and painter, Bénédictus was innately receptive to accidents, so investigated. He discovered that the beaker had contained cellulose nitrate, which had held the shards of glass together. He quickly spotted the potential of glass that broke but didn't shatter; his safety glass first appeared in World War One gas masks, then in windscreens, and soon became ubiquitous.

Vulcanised rubber was discovered by accident by Charles Goodyear. Rubber was too soft when hot and too brittle when cold. Goodyear accidentally spilled some rubber on his stove. It baked into a hard dark substance, strong and pliable at any temperature. He had discovered the process of vulcanisation by accident, but he used the accident to his advantage. He is considered to be the patron saint of inventors because these days rubber is present in almost every mechanical object.

The electric current was discovered by accident by Galvani, as was immunology by Pasteur, X-rays by Röntgen, photography by Daguerre, radioactivity by Becquerel and penicillin by Fleming.

Become a student of the University of Accidents. When they invented the computer, they also invented the computer crash. The printer, the blotchy print. Every technology carries with it the potential for accident. Work with them and explore them. Accidents generate new perspectives. They appeal to the creative mind because we live in an imperfect world, we are imperfect and our work is imperfect.

Accidents reflect reality more accurately than does perfection. Perfection is the aberration. Think of an accident as an answer in search of a different question. Work out what that different question is. It is probably more interesting than the one you were asking.

'There is no such thing as accident; it is fate misnamed.'

Napoleon Bonaparte

Inspired? *Embrace the art of imperfection on p. 65, or turn over to meet the world's most successful failure.*

if you can't be really good, be really bad

I've watched the films of Ed Wood over and over again. *Bride of the Monster*, *Plan 9 from Outer Space* and *Night of the Ghouls* are unbelievable. Unbelievably bad. They are also some of the poorest-quality and strangest films ever made. The critics lashed every film he released during his lifetime and they were all box-office failures, but his zeal for making movies remained undimmed. Wood created a remarkable number of films. He raised the finance, produced, wrote, directed and acted in them, often simultaneously. On film after film he worked with the reckless enthusiasm of a child, with nothing dampening his spirit. You forgive even his worst films because he still manages to convey his love for the trashy characters, plots and sets. Lesser men, if forced to make movies under the conditions Wood faced, would have given up.

Wood's posthumous fame began when he was awarded the accolade of 'Worst Director of All Time' in 1980, just two years after his death. Today, his films are celebrated for their technical mistakes, wobbly sets, unsophisticated special effects, eccentric dialogue, peculiar casts and bizarre plots.

These features add charm, character and a zany spirit that are more enduring than the blockbusters churned out by Hollywood. Wood's beguiling films have the rare attributes of sincerity and humanity that most hi-tech, high-budget sci-fi films lack. They were produced for a pittance with untrained actors and you sense that everyone involved was driven by commitment, not money.

Something badly done can be refreshing. Being prepared to be uncool or nerdy can be charming. It's a way of showing that you don't care what anyone else thinks. The world is full of people who dedicate their lives to seeking approval. They chase after vindication from others and lose themselves in the process. They try to produce something that earns kudos rather than something they really enjoy. Aiming for critical credibility or commercial success can be vastly more limiting than relying on passion and enthusiasm, the engine that powers creativity.

AuctionWeb was a bad website. People posted badly lit, unfocused photos of junk they wanted to sell. A 24/7 world-wide garage sale. It was horrible to scroll through the visually appalling photos. One of the first items sold was a broken laser pointer for $14.83. Astonished, the founder of the site, Pierre Omidyar, emailed the winning bidder to ask if he understood that the laser pointer was broken. The buyer explained in his reply, 'I'm a collector of broken laser point-ers.' That's when Omidyar realised he was onto something.

He had founded AuctionWeb in California in 1995. It soon changed its name to eBay. eBay became one of the great new technology companies of the last twenty-five years *because* it was bad and unashamedly uncool. Omidyar poured his enthusiasm into it and made it work well, but he didn't try to make it chic or sophisticated.

Too much self-criticism can paralyse you and stop you moving forward. People with mediocre ideas and poor taste often achieve exceptional success because they don't know when to stop. Better the errors of enthusiasm than the slick competence of the cool.

'Success is the ability to go from failure to failure without losing your enthusiasm.'

Winston Churchill

Disagree? Discover the merits of feeling inadequate on p. 43.

be a conservative revolutionary

An elegant model strutted down the catwalk in high heels. She wore a gracefully tailored white cotton muslin dress with white synthetic tulle underskirt. The audience contained the fashion world's most elite representatives. They were stunned when, halfway down the catwalk, the model was attacked from both sides. Coloured paint was sprayed across her dress in overlapping streaks. The model's face was spattered and paint dribbled down her dress onto the floor. Why?

It was all staged by the enfant terrible of fashion design, Alexander McQueen, for his spring/summer collection. The audience literally screamed their ovation and *Dress, No. 13*, spring/summer 1999 is now a fashion icon.

It's important not to do the same old things in the same old way, but to push them to the limit and see what happens if you are excessive. For decades models had strutted up and down the catwalks of Paris and Milan parading the season's new fashions. It was the convention. Alexander McQueen smashed those expectations.

McQueen was the most iconic and celebrated fashion designer of the nineteen-nineties. His mesmerising outfits and otherworldly designs became instant classics. McQueen amplified his abilities with dramatic catwalk shows that transformed fashion shows into performance art. Instead of simply marching models up and down a catwalk, McQueen's shows were sensational events. Not content with being the greatest fashion designer of his time, he wanted a wider audience. He wanted everyone to notice, not just the fashion world.

McQueen drew attention to his phenomenal tailoring skills and unique design concepts with provocative catwalk shows. He thought big. He ignored practicalities. No matter how outrageous his vision, on however small a budget, it was always realised: rain pouring onto the catwalk, wolves terrorising the audience, fire leaping from the floor, models ice-skating, models as ethereal holograms in glass pyramids, recreations of shipwrecks and mental asylums. He raised the bar on what fashion shows could be. He turned them into unmissable events.

The American painter Mark Rothko was similarly excessive. His first one-man exhibition in New York was of portraits of his friends. They were ordinary. So he began to push painting to the limit. He put all his efforts into what he was good at – shape, colour and composition. His paintings became more and more abstract. Eventually he and the other abstract expressionists started producing paintings that were *entirely* abstract, an expression of pure feeling and nothing more. Until then, paintings had always been based on something in the real world.

Rothko developed paintings based on rectangular blocks of two to three complementary colours. The blocks vibrate and resonate against the surrounding area. The monumental canvases overwhelm and completely envelop the viewer. His paintings express basic human emotions – tragedy, ecstasy and doom. Many observers find viewing his paintings such a moving experience they weep when standing in front of them. Viewers describe feeling something close to the deep spiritual experience Rothko claimed to have while painting them.

Rothko, who became one of the most important abstract expressionists, found the thing he was good at simply by being as excessive as possible. Many people never connect with their real talents and fail to attain their potential because they don't push what they do to excess. Creativity is like mining; we need to dig deep to discover and uncover ourselves.

Whatever your field, look at the systems you work within and see what happens if you are excessive. It will make your work stand out, and remind you that one person who is prepared to be excessive can achieve more in an hour than fifty reasonable people can achieve in a year.

'If you aren't in over your head, how do you know how tall you are?'

T.S. Eliot

Meet another conservative revolutionary who was full of contradictions on p. 220.

raise the dead

Can you guess which film is described below?

An orphaned boy, our hero, lives with his aunt and uncle in the middle of nowhere. Their life is tedious, boring and unexciting and he longs for something more.

Our hero's life is turned upside down one day when a strange character arrives to tell him the truth about his background, parents and true potential. He discovers that his parents were special and that he, too, can learn special powers.

A bearded, elderly guardian, who knows his full history but is not prepared to reveal everything, mentors our hero. The guardian rescued him as a baby and delivered him to his aunt and uncle to hide the child from evil forces.

The boy is taught to use his extraordinary powers; he manifests them through a special stick. Only select people have these powers, which enable them to do extraordinary things.

Our hero learns that there exists an embodiment of evil, who murdered his parents. He is the master of dark powers; he intends to rule the world and will do anything to make that happen. His minions work hard to spread his evil.

Our hero declares that he will never be tempted by the power of evil and sets out on a quest to destroy it. Along the way he befriends two loyal, trusted sidekicks, one male – emotional and headstrong – and the other female – smart and astute. Later they are to fall in love with each other. Our hero overcomes immense dangers to save his friends and we begin to realise the great future ahead of him.

In the end, the embodiment of evil is defeated by a greater power – love.

It could be *Star Wars* or Harry Potter. With a bit of tweaking it could be a lot of other films too. The similarity doesn't diminish their power or, strangely, their originality. I'm a huge fan of *Star Wars* and have watched it tens of times. My loft is full of the original toys. I am a big fan of Harry Potter and have watched the films tens of times. My loft is full of the original toys. I queued with my children late at night to get the books on first release, have read them several times and have spent many hours listening to the audiotapes read by Stephen Fry. I never tired of the storyline, even though I already knew it from *Star Wars*.

All creative work builds on what has gone before. When someone declares something is original, it's because they are unaware of the influences. The creative make the most of things they admire, and aren't ashamed to be inspired by something they respect. The bad news: everything has already been done. The good news: hardly anyone noticed, so it can be done again.

The plot of Stephenie Meyer's *Twilight* was inspired by *Wuthering Heights*, but quickly deviates from Emily Brontë's classic. *The Wide Sargasso Sea* by Jean Rhys was a creative response to Charlotte Brontë's *Jane Eyre*. Rhys was so entranced by the book, that she wanted the characters to be developed further and created a prequel that fills in the characters' backstories, and gave the character Bertha a voice that she lacked in the original. Stravinsky cut up the music of Pergolesi, Tchaikovsky and the folk music that he enjoyed and collaged them into new work.

If the action of *Moby-Dick* by Herman Melville was set today, what would it be like? Swap the white whale for a white shark and you can see where the inspiration for Peter Benchley's novel and Steven Spielberg's film *Jaws* originated. In *Moby-Dick* Captain Ahab searches for a ferocious white whale, which has wreaked widespread destruction. Moby-Dick has the human characteristic of revenge and this drives him to ruthlessly attack humans. Ahab pursues and finds the whale, but he rams and sinks his boat. Moby-Dick spins the boat round and Ahab is dragged into the depths by the whale.

Peter Benchley and Steven Spielberg admired *Moby-Dick* and reinvented it for modern times. A great story was reinvigorated for a contemporary audience and made relevant again. They took a classic and pushed it further. *Moby-Dick* served as a starting point for them to add even more interesting ideas and themes.

'*Jaws* on a spaceship.' That was all Ridley Scott said when he pitched the film *Alien* to producers at 20th Century Fox. That was all he needed to say. They instantly understood. They were well aware of the impact of *Jaws* and now it was set in a confined space with nowhere to run. Pitching a film is difficult: you're trying to persuade the studio to give you millions to hire scriptwriters, actors, set designers and the rest of the team and you have nothing to show, just an idea.

'*Jaws* on a spaceship' was a concept the production team could refer back to. The casting director knew to cast unknown actors because the cast of *Jaws* were unknown at the time and were easier for the public to identify with than Hollywood stars. The small ship, the *Orca* in *Jaws*, was rickety and malfunctioning, as was the spaceship the *Nostromo* in *Alien*. It was completely unlike the sleek, ultra-modern ships seen before in films such as *Star Wars* and *2001: A Space Odyssey*. In *Jaws*, you only see glimpses of the shark; you don't see the whole monster until the end. That helped to disguise the fact that it was a model. They used the same technique in *Alien* to conceal the fact that the monster was a man in a rubber suit. There are numerous similarities, but Ridley Scott and his team transformed the core idea of *Jaws* into something unique and original as they added their own concepts. *Jaws* was the scaffolding Scott could use to build his own house. *Alien* has spawned a hundred copies, and so it goes on.

The creative often remake a story, painting, idea or song that impresses them. In the remaking it becomes theirs and they transform it into something totally new. If a work by someone else really gets into your head, sometimes you have to remake it yourself, simply to get it back out of your head.

'There is no harm in repeating a good thing.'

Plato

Not interested in reworking your own ideas? *Rework your idols', on p. 195.*

work the hours that work for you

Scientists in the Theoretical Division of the Los Alamos National Laboratory were troubled when their brilliant colleague Mitchell Feigenbaum began living by a twenty-six-hour clock instead of the traditional twenty-four-hour one. His days went in and out of phase with theirs – he periodically woke up to a setting sun, or had breakfast when they were having supper.

Feigenbaum was studying chaos and wanted randomness in everyday life. During his twenty-six-hour day he didn't think about traditional scientific problems; he thought about clouds, the smoke swirls from cigarettes and whirlpools, which were structured yet unpredictable. His colleagues thought he was wasting his gifts, but he became the man most responsible for chaos theory, the study of randomness in a system that also obeys laws. No other recent theoretical science has had such a phenomenal impact on our culture.

Chaos posed problems that flouted established scientific methods. Only someone like Feigenbaum, who lived differently and therefore thought differently, could have discovered chaos theory.

To think and act creatively you cannot live by timetables. The world revolves around schedules, but routines create routine behaviour, and routine behaviour creates routine thinking. Routine is not organisation. Organisation is a successful arrangement. Routine is mindless repetition.

Working at night is magical. Surrounded by dark and silence we can access a world closed to others. It's like another planet. The writer Craig Clevenger seals himself in his house for days when starting a new novel. He covers all the clocks and windows with black duct tape and foil in order to lose all sense of the passage of time. Nobel Prize-winning writer Toni Morrison started writing before dawn, but by necessity rather than by choice, as her young children woke at 5 a.m. Charles Dickens walked the streets at night and met in the docks, markets and backstreets of London strange characters who resurfaced in his novels.

Be wary of normal patterns and schedules: they produce normal and regular thinking. Rip up timetables and disrupt routines. If you are truly involved in your work, ten hours can feel like ten minutes, whereas most people are working in jobs where ten minutes feels like ten hours. If you are fascinated by and totally involved in what you're doing you become lost in the moment and perform at your peak. Work the hours that work for you.

'If you want to change your art, change your habits.'

Clement Greenberg

Not quite convinced? *Become immersed in the moment on p. 100.*

search without finding

I watched the most mysterious and enigmatic man I've ever seen stride across the room. He emerged from nowhere and was going nowhere. His thin limbs seemed to stretch out endlessly and gave him a fragile appearance, yet he exuded inner strength. Six foot tall, he leaned forward with determination and seemed knowing, yet tentative and questioning. A universal man encapsulating our times.

Walking Man 1 was a 1960 bronze sculpture by Alberto Giacometti that strode into the record books in 2010 when it sold for $104.3 million. Giacometti was an artist who felt he could never capture another person in paint or plaster because people are too unfathomable and complex. When painting or sculpting, Giacometti searched but never found. More importantly, he enjoyed that state of ignorance. It was a release. There was more freedom in it than knowing, than being certain. He worked from real life, yet believed it was not possible to capture reality in a painting or likeness in a portrait. Light always fluctuated and both he and his sitters always moved, if only imperceptibly. Everything visible was unstable and changeable. That meant it was impossible to produce a static two-dimensional painting of what we see. He was wise enough to understand that he could only ever try, but never truly capture reality.

Don't be ashamed of being ignorant. Ignorance is natural. Creativity exists in not knowing. You have to be happy to admit that you are ignorant and may never find a solution. Even thinking there is an answer is a trap, a dead end. Be willing to look stupid, to risk the emotional pain of getting it wrong.

When the Delphic Oracle declared the philosopher Socrates the wisest person in Greece, he suggested that it was because he realised how little he knew. He also realised how little everyone else knew! Socrates didn't have a philosophy and didn't write anything down; he simply asked his followers questions. He considered it a success if, at the end of a session with him, his followers knew less than at the beginning.

If you don't know what you're doing, you don't know what you can't do. You must search for answers without needing to find them. There is freedom in ignorance, whereas knowledge is a full stop. Use what you've learned to create a higher-quality ignorance. You have to be fully conscious of how ignorant you are before you can stride forward with determination and uncertainty.

'Painting to me is constant searching. I can see what I want, but I can't get there, and yet you have to be open enough that if it goes another way, then let it go that way.'

Jamie Wyeth

More? Embrace the certainty of doubt on p. 40.

don't overlook the overlooked

After reading a newspaper account of the murder of farmer Herbert Clutter, his wife and children in 1959, American writer Truman Capote decided to investigate. He made the 1,700 km journey to the crime scene, River Valley Farm. It was picturesque and tranquil, with a white angular roof jutting out of a swirling a sea of corn and surrounded by elm trees. It languished outside a small town in Kansas, the tight-knit heartland of Middle America. The Clutters were decent, hard-working and gentle. The killers were the dark side of America: rootless, impetuous and irreverent. This contrast fascinated Capote. He wanted to understand as deeply as possible the motives and characters of everyone involved. He saturated himself in the incident, interviewing local residents, police appointed to the case and the killers before their executions. After six years he had compiled 8,000 pages of notes, which became the basis for his award-winning non-fiction classic *In Cold Blood*.

The book was an instant sensation and is now considered a classic of American reportage. Indeed Capote had created a new genre, an original form: the 'non-fiction novel'. It was neither a whodunnit nor a will-they-be-caught because those questions were answered at the beginning. Instead, its fascination lay in other things: getting into the minds of those involved and discovering what made them tick; exploring the dynamics between the murderers and their victims; and the suspense of reading to the end to find out the gory details.

The intriguing and compelling surround us, but we don't notice them. There are reports of murders in most newspapers, most days. We flick through them and they barely register. We are distracted by irrelevant nonsense. Creativity can be as simple as seizing on something that has been overlooked by the world and forcing it to take notice.

We are all missing opportunities all the time. Those opportunities are in the astounding objects, characters, views and stories that surround us. They are under our noses, but most people overlook them. If your mind is alert to your surroundings and the strangeness in the commonplace, you can make the most of whatever is already out there. Use anything interesting that you find.

'Nothing exists until or unless it is observed. An artist is making something exist by observing it.'

William Burroughs

Find natural inspiration in the everyday on p. 46.

put the right thing
in the wrong place

How can you refresh your perspective and see things in a new light? Put something or someone in an unusual place. Looking at your subject in an unexpected location throws off the preconceptions and stereotypes you have of them. By putting everyday things where we would not expect, extraordinary potential is revealed.

Surrealist artists invented the simple technique of putting two different objects together to create unusual juxtapositions. During the nineteen-thirties, Salvador Dalí's lobster telephone, in which a replica lobster replaced the receiver of a telephone, changed the way designers thought about product design. It was fully functioning. Dalí understood that everyday things had a meaning beyond their practical function. We are surrounded by objects that are the legacy of his vision of combining unusual objects, from phones shaped like burgers or bananas through to baby buggies – the latter another reminder that putting two unusual objects together can unleash huge potential.

Owen Maclaren designed the undercarriage of the Spitfire, the British fighter plane that dominated the skies during the Battle of Britain. Its undercarriage folded up in a neat but complex way. In 1965 Maclaren invented a collapsible buggy inspired by this folding mechanism and it revolutionised the transportation of babies and small children; previously, prams and pushchairs had been heavy, rigid and impractical. Owen went into production with the new lightweight aluminium Maclaren Baby Buggy in 1967. It sold millions in tens of countries. Maclaren also inspired future collapsible objects such as the Strida bicycle.

Bill Gates had a policy at Microsoft of taking an employee and putting them in a completely different department for a while so that ideas from one area were transferred to another. He did it just to see what happened. Sometimes it produced nothing but occasionally it produced amazing results.

Put disparate people and things together, not for any purpose, but to see what happens. Whatever your field, put your subject in different contexts. It's not what you look at that matters, it's what you see.

'The man who cannot visualise a horse galloping on a tomato is an idiot.'

André Breton

Inspired? *Try going from A to B via Z on p. 232.*

stay hungry

We crave luxury, but it's a motivational sedative. It's a hindrance. It saps us of incentive. It whispers to our unconscious mind to relax, to take it easy. Neutral, simple, humble spaces are what help us to focus. Luxury is not for the creative; it's for poodles.

The most uncompromising portrait painter of his era, Lucian Freud, kept his studio bare, empty and free of distractions. Freud forged his closest bonds in his studio. His sitters – duchesses, drag queens, queens, his partners and children – never forgot the intense experience. There was . nothing else to concentrate on other than the experience of painting and being painted.

Freud was unsparing in his depictions of the truths of human flesh. His paintings were solely about the authenticity of his own vision. Facts are one thing; the truth is another. It's more revealing. To get to the truth Freud needed a pared-down environment. All his models, however beautiful or grotesque, were subjected to the same austere interrogation. He painted them as he saw them, describing blemishes and flaws with none of the customary flattery of portrait painters. He invested everything in the painting. The point is that he was not dependent on anything. He needed no crutches – no music, phone, no airs or graces, nothing.

Freud worked long hours – a morning session with one model, an afternoon break and an evening session with another model – seven days a week, all year round. He cut himself off from the clamour of the city. He stayed alert and fresh because he was isolated from the nonsense of everyday life.

Freud did not lead a monastic life. At a drinking club called the Colony Room, for every sip I took of my drink, he'd down a glass. He frequently got into fights. He had a lot of children with many different partners. He lived life to the full. It was different in his studio, though; there he needed a clear mental space.

Ralph Waldo Emerson, Emily Dickinson, Henry David Thoreau and others too numerous to mention have all sought solitude to find a rich vein of inspiration. A sparse office or studio keeps the brain sharp. You become completely absorbed and able to see things for what they are. Scattered forces become directed into one powerful channel. The mind wants to wander. Keep it on track by eliminating sidetracks.

'The saddest thing I can imagine is to get used to luxury.'

Charlie Chaplin

See why Einstein favoured a messy workspace on p. 192.

surprise yourself

You may not realise it, but you have an interesting story to tell. A must-hear tale. We all do. A struggle against illness, family hardship, poverty or a sudden breakthrough moment. Whether we are aware of it or not, our life is our subject matter, and freeing up our memories allows us to surprise ourselves and learn about our personalities and what makes us so unique. Everything is self-expression; we create our biographies in everything we do.

Artist Frida Kahlo made the most of the events of her life. Her iconic status is due to her small, autobiographical paintings. Although technically poor and crude, they are fascinating because they tell her enthralling story. Her optimism and boundless enthusiasm were not affected by the tragic events of her life. At the age of six she was stricken with polio, which left her with a deformed foot and a limp. Later in life she suffered serious injuries to her right leg and pelvis in a traffic accident and faced a lifelong battle against pain. During her convalescence she painted her first self-portrait, the beginning of a lengthy series that mapped her emotional reactions to events in her life. Kahlo's injuries meant she could not have children and she documented her miscarriages in paintings. She met the artist Diego Rivera and they embarked on a turbulent marriage. Kahlo underwent many operations on her spine and her crippled foot; at one point, threatened by gangrene, her right leg was amputated below the knee: a huge blow to someone so preoccupied with self-image. She learned to walk again with an artificial limb. All these events are chronicled in her paintings. She is her own subject matter.

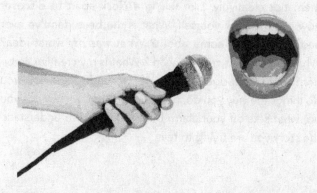

Although Kahlo's later paintings became clumsy and chaotic due to the joint effects of pain, drugs and drink, they were her finest work and her artistic reputation grew. They explained and documented her life. The paintings show that she decided not to be a victim. All the pain she suffered did not prevent her from having a love affair with life.

Howard Schultz was best known as the CEO of Starbucks. His father struggled with a series of blue-collar jobs, never able to find meaning or satisfaction in his work. Then he was injured at work and had no health insurance or worker's compensation. It left a lasting impression on Schultz. 'It was not the calling of coffee, but the calling to try to build a company that my father never got a chance to work for,' he said. He believed Starbucks was the first company in America to offer comprehensive health insurance and ownership in the form of stock options to all its employees. His negative experience proved to be positive for his company.

Everyone needs to analyse and understand what makes them tick creatively. Like taking a clock apart to discover how it works. Ask yourself, What is the best idea I've ever had? How did it come about? What was my worst idea? What was my first creative work? What is my creative ambition? Self-knowledge will help you to understand why you do things the way you do, how you function, what winds you up, what sets off your alarm bell. You'll start to understand the story you are trying to tell.

'All art is autobiographical. The pearl is the oyster's autobiography.'

Federico Fellini

Meet another artist who used her own experience to make an impression on p. 18.

take advantage of a disadvantage

The extraordinary achievements of Chuck Close, the great photorealist artist, are a fascinating example of turning a disadvantage into an advantage. His huge, painstakingly accurate portrait paintings hang in every major museum in the world. The monumental scale is breathtaking. Standing before them is like standing in front of a mountain. The minute details astound and amaze; yet they pull together to make a towering portrait. Close spent insane amounts of time on the microscopic details in his images.

Catastrophe struck Close at the height of his fame. A blood clot in the spine left him paralysed from the neck down. Close had been known for detailed brushwork, and now suddenly he couldn't even hold a brush. As Jackson Pollock said, 'Painting is no problem. The problem is what to do when you're not painting.'

After intensive rehabilitation Close regained slight move-ment in his arm. He learned to paint again with a paintbrush strapped to his wrist with tape. Eventually he could manipulate a brush well enough to create tiny abstract shapes. He went on to create an entirely new kind of portrait: small abstract squares that, viewed close up, are separate, swirling marks, but which seen from a distance coalesce like pixels into a single, mosaic-like, unified image. The colours were stronger and brighter. These paintings were even more popular and cemented Close's place in art history. The way Close reacted to the ravages of ill health had miraculously transformed him into one of the great colourists.

Close did not let the handicap stop him doing what he felt he had been born to do. He turned the disadvantage of his disability into a source of innovation. Perhaps his tough early life had trained him to turn disadvantages to his favour: his father died when he was eleven and soon after his mother became ill and the medical bills cost them their house. Close had dyslexia and suffered at school, where he was considered dumb and lazy. He was told he would never go to college, and yet he went to Yale. He overcame every obstacle.

In 1980, the great jazz guitarist Pat Martino suffered a severe brain aneurysm and underwent an operation. The surgery made him suffer complete amnesia; Martino couldn't remember his family and friends, how to play the guitar, his career or even who he was. He felt he'd been 'dropped cold, empty, neutral, cleansed . . . naked'. For months he exhaustively studied his old recordings, and in time managed to reverse his memory loss and return to form on the guitar. His past recordings were 'an old friend, a spiritual experi- ence which remained beautiful and honest'. In the early nineteen-nineties, he resumed his performing. His experiences added a new dimension to his playing.

Many regard Django Reinhardt as one of the greatest guitar players of all time because he invented an entirely new style of jazz called 'hot' jazz guitar. He had to: the fingers on his left hand were burned in a fire and paralysed. Reinhardt could only use the index and middle fingers. In overcoming this problem he created a musical tradition and his most popular compositions have become jazz standards.

These creative thinkers not only overcame their disadvantages but actively used them to add a new dimension to their work. You have to try to see a setback as an opportunity to begin again with more wisdom; then you too can overcome seemingly insurmountable misfortunes. 'I must do something' always resolves more problems than 'Something must be done.'

'Adversity has the effect of eliciting talents, which in prosperous circumstances would have lain dormant.'

Horace

Prefer classical to jazz? Meet another musician who turned adversity to their advantage on p. 187.

throw truth bombs

The truth has power, and therefore gives your work strength. It is often unpalatable – possibly even offensive. You must not sacrifice the truth to be inoffensive. To produce something that will stand the test of time, it's important to reveal something or uncover something hidden.

The Impressionists revealed the truth about the optics of the eye and the perception of space. The Futurists revealed the truth about how the modern world was all about speed, travelling quickly and information flowing swiftly. The Surrealists revealed the truth about the importance of the subconscious and how our true desires were hidden from view. Pop Artists revealed the truth about the effects of consumer society and capitalism on our values. Conceptual artists revealed the truth about the dominance of ideas in our perception of the world. Galileo spent the latter years of his life under house arrest for revealing that the Earth was not the centre of the universe but revolved round the Sun. They were all searching for the real meaning of the world around them.

We live in a world of PR, image-makers, shifting identities and media consultants. Most people are trying to hide the truth, to cover things up and project a false image. The truly creative person seeks to reveal and not to conceal. They tell the truth about the truth. What is the real, below-the-surface reason you are interested in your subject?

'All truths are easy to understand once they are discovered; the point is to discover them.'

Galileo

Inspired? Try Shock and Awe, p. 152.
Uninspired? Find out why the truth isn't always sufficient on p. 256.

suspend judgement

I sat in the Royal Albert Hall, along with a few thousand other music fans, completely riveted. Some had travelled hundreds of miles to be there. The historical setting contributed to the compelling atmosphere. The virtuoso pianist walked onstage, lifted the lid of his piano and sat there in silence for four minutes and thirty-three seconds with a seriousness of purpose that was palpable to us all. Then he closed the lid of the piano and walked offstage. We had listened excitedly to nothing. The audience and orchestra behind the pianist sat still, a violinist dropped his bow, an oboist rustled as he stretched his leg and there was an unintentional wind solo from the stomach of a woman sitting two rows in front of me, but that was all. When the piece came to an end, the conductor said, 'And now for some real music,' and proceeded with the programme of Brahms and Beethoven. What a philistine.

We had listened to John Cage's '4'33"'. It was performed without the pianist playing a single note. The piece consisted of the sounds in the auditorium: coughs, clothes rustling, breathing and distant sounds of traffic. *4'33"* made the point that all sound is equally valid. The sound of a Beethoven symphony is no more beautiful than that of a food mixer. It is not necessarily what we listen to that is significant, but listening itself. What makes *4'33"* so compelling is the simplicity of the concept.

Cage tried to eliminate judgement from music because he believed that everything was music and that the sound of traffic was as beautiful as a Mozart concerto. Music didn't just exist in concert halls but was all around us, all the time. Which means we are all in the best seats. In a way, he was pointing out that we all only hear what we listen to. He simply listened harder than most.

To get the most out of any situation it is important to suspend judgement. We judge everything: people, prices, products, behaviour; and automatically categorise things as 'good' or 'bad'. Once you have pigeonholed something, it is locked down. Deferring judgement keeps all possibilities open.

Try to abandon conventional criteria like the one that holds that traditional forms of art are more beautiful than anything else. Throw away hierarchies and accept that everything has qualities of some kind and you have opened yourself up to the beauty of all things.

Judgement and creativity are two different processes. It is important to create freely, and it is not possible to do that and judge at the same time. Defer forming opinions or jumping to conclusions until the end of the process.

'Look. Art knows no prejudice, art knows no boundaries, art doesn't really have judgement in its purest form. So just go, just go.'

k.d.lang

Convinced? Open your mind with Andy Warhol on p. 103.
Not convinced? Try searching high and low on p. 175.

throw yourself into yourself

If you are not doing what you want, what are you doing?

Surely it follows that you must be doing what you don't want to do. You're probably doing what others want you to do. Give yourself permission instead to follow what excites and intrigues you. This is how you can get the most out of yourself.

The novelist James Joyce did not compromise – he wrote in whatever way he wanted. His talents did not suit traditional academic writing so he made the most of his experimental writing abilities. He did not take into account the reader or the market potential of his writing. He made no concessions. He wrote in his own unique style. The result was *Ulysses*, a turning point in modern literature. It presents the unedited, uncensored stream-of-consciousness thoughts of a fictitious character. There are long chaotic passages, strange words and obscure allusions. Many consider it the greatest book ever written. Others consider it the worst; it was even banned for many years. Whatever: the novel is exactly what Joyce wanted. He indulged himself and completely disregarded the readers and critics. He was not striving for something outside himself, such as critical acclaim or high sales figures. He was not concerned with worldly ambitions, and this is why, paradoxically, *Ulysses* became an enduring classic.

Our society believes that work must be hard and unfulfilling. The important things many of us really want to do – dance, act, paint, write – must be frivolous because they are enjoyable. A talent for acting, music or poetry is not taken seriously because it appears to be too satisfying, too enjoyable.

A student on one of my workshops was not doing what she wanted to do. She worked in the admin department of her company but wanted to work in the marketing department, producing adverts. She felt her creativity was going unappreciated. She wanted to resign. She had applied to transfer to the marketing department but had been frequently rebuffed. I explained that she needed to 'do' the marketing. Up until now she had tried to persuade her superiors with words. Words disappear the moment they are said. She needed to *show* them. I got her to do an advertising campaign for her company. She came up with the concept, wrote the strapline, took the photos, designed the layouts – the whole shebang. It was better than the advertising campaign her company had just done. She showed her superiors. They moved her to the marketing department immediately. They could *see* that she was more suited to marketing.

If you are totally self-indulgent you will be at your best. You will be doing what you care about most. Think enjoyment. Think pleasure. Do what you most want to do. It's better for you. It's better for everyone. If you are satisfied, your satisfaction spreads to others.

'A man is a success if he gets up in the morning and goes to bed at night and in between does what he wants to do.'

Bob Dylan

More? *Follow Robert De Niro and create your own opportunities on p. 22.*

use shock and awe

The haphazard rows of razor-sharp teeth loomed out at me through the murky green liquid. I could see past them into the large black hole of its monstrous gullet. Its cold, black eyes stared at me and I stared back into the face of death.

I first saw *The Physical Impossibility of Death in the Mind of Someone Living* by Damien Hirst at the Saatchi Gallery in London in 1992. It was an artwork that dominated the era, a 4.3m real shark preserved in a huge glass tank filled with formaldehyde. The viewer stood a few inches away from the gaping jaws of a fully grown shark. It created a disturbingly immediate, and visceral experience. The shark brought you face to face with life and death. Hirst didn't want a painting of a shark. He wanted a real shark, real enough to frighten, to force the viewer out of their comfort zone. The work explores our greatest fears. You're forced to think about death. It doesn't give you any choice; you have to confront your darkest nightmares.

In the creative world shock for the sake of shock is justifiable, since it forces us to ask *why* we are shocked. Stirring others out of their complacency can be good for everyone. The role of the scientist is generally to reassure, to establish certainty, to correct error. The role of the creative is to disturb, question and unsettle. The creative mind reveals deeper, more fundamental truths than mere facts.

It is common practice for directors to sneak into cinemas when their film has just been released to see the audience's reaction. When Steven Spielberg's *Jaws* previewed in cinemas in 1975, he took a dose of Valium and stood anxiously at the back of a screening in Dallas. He flicked his gaze between the audience and the screen. After the scene where a boy on a raft is killed, a man in the front row stood up, ran out past Spielberg, threw up all over the carpet in the lobby, went to the bathroom to clean up and then returned to his seat. 'That's when I knew I had a hit,' said Spielberg.

If you haven't got the attention of your audience, you're talking to yourself. A vending machine in a shopping mall drew a great deal of attention; it displayed rows of shiny new pistols instead of chocolate bars or cans of drink. On close inspection, they turned out to be real. It was as easy to buy guns as sweets. You are urged to put money in the slot because, 'Your donation will go to the Gun Control Alliance, for a gun-free South Africa.' A line explained, 'This is how easy it is to get hold of a gun in South Africa.' We're used to government posters warning us about this or that. We turn off. That ambient advertising campaign had impact. Of course you couldn't get a gun from the machine, but it made the point that in South Africa you could buy a gun just as easily as you would buy a chocolate bar.

The roots of shock run deep into the history of culture. The real currency of our time is not money; it's attention. You need everyone's attention in order to deliver a message of substance. New ideas will always shock. Don't let the reaction of others unnerve you.

'The undoubted shock, even disgust, provoked by the work is part of its appeal.'

Nicholas Serota

More? *Stand erect and make what you say unforgettable on p. 209.*

Less? *Let poor Rachmaninov remind you that sometimes it takes longer than we'd like to be appreciated on p. 161.*

value obscurity

If you feel overlooked, that no one is interested in what you're doing, enjoy the moment. Obscurity is a creative place: you are free to experiment and fail. No one is watching. No one has any expectations. Entrepreneurs, designers, writers and artists make the most of the freedom obscurity offers.

Kurt Cobain and his band, Nirvana, produced the classic, multimillion-selling album *Nevermind*, one of the most influential records of all time. Its far-reaching legacy is still as potent today as ever. Its strange combination of hard-edged rock, catchy melodies, dynamic shifts from quiet to loud and Cobain's raw, angst-ridden voice sound as fresh today as when they were recorded.

Nirvana were virtually unknown when they recorded *Nevermind*. In obscurity, Cobain revelled in the thrill of finding his own voice, of creating a new language to speak to the world with. He experimented with guitar and vocal techniques for the sheer hell of it. Often homeless, he claimed he sometimes resorted to living under a bridge. It was a fraught but exciting time. He was discovering what to say and how to say it. There was no pressure. He had all the time he needed to experiment and discover who he was and what he wanted to express.

After fame came his way, an army of people suddenly relied on Cobain: the other band members, the record company, manager, roadies, retailers, accountants, journalists, PAs and fans. Hundreds of magazines and TV stations clamoured for interviews. They all wanted a stake in him. He quickly began to miss obscurity. Before the straitjacket of fame there was just Kurt, only one person to worry about. Now, he bought an expensive, gigantic multi-roomed mansion, but slept in a cheap motel nearby. He was trying to recapture the early sense of freedom. He wanted to develop, to experiment and try new ideas, but no one else wanted that. They wanted another *Nevermind*, and another, and another. Cobain came to realise that his anonymity had been precious.

Obscurity is a time to be savoured. If you're lucky enough to be in obscurity, make the most of it. If you're a CEO, every decision you make is analysed and scrutinised. If you're lower down the ranks you can try things out and fail. Success brings the weight of expectations and pressure that can do far more harm than good.

'I'm afraid of losing my obscurity. Genuineness only thrives in the dark. Like celery.'

Aldous Huxley

If you liked obscurity, you'll love anonymity on p. 204.
Alternatively, consider making yourself the story on p. 37.

if something doesn't need improving, improve it

Martin and Allyson Egbert set out on a quest to find an alternative treatment for their son. He was born with congenital clubfoot, a rare but crippling deformity of the foot. The standard treatment in the late nineteen-nineties seems barbaric today: years of painful surgical operations that left the feet scarred and stiff. Surely there was a better way? The Egberts phoned, surfed the Internet, asked questions and probed.

They discovered an overlooked treatment created in the nineteen-forties by Dr Ignacio Ponseti. Ponseti had studied the anatomy of the foot and developed a non-surgical technique that manipulated the baby's feet when they were young and flexible, then held them in place with a plaster cast for a short while. It was highly effective and left children with perfectly normal feet.

Despite the clear advantages of the Ponseti Method, and the unequivocal clinical evidence of its effectiveness, it met with opposition. A surgical technique was being transformed into a non-surgical technique. Surgeons were locked into a 'We-have-always-done-it-this-way' inertia. There was a lot of prestige and status attached to being a surgeon and they wanted to keep it that way. Surgeons were proud of their skills and here was someone telling them that surgery was not the best remedy. They continued to cut ligaments, lengthen tendons, open joints, pin bones and do irreparable damage. Tens of thousands of children underwent needlessly painful operations. Ponseti's situation is common to people who produce something groundbreaking: they're surrounded by people who at best are resistant to new ideas, and at worst wilfully ignore them.

The Egberts visited the retired Dr Ponseti to ask him to correct their baby's clubfoot. On their way home, they determined to start a website to explain the technique to other parents. Eventually the Ponseti Method gained acceptance and dramatically changed thousands of lives. It took someone outside the medical profession to see clearly, and to find the better way.

Search for a better method when everyone else is content with the standard. Hierarchies maintain the quo after it's lost its status. There is always a better way. We are often trapped into prescribed methods because that's how things have always been done. We go along with what is normal, when we should always be looking to extend and improve. You must always challenge and question tried-and-tested methods. There is always space for improvement, no matter how long you've been doing the same thing the same way.

'Iteration, like friction, is likely to generate heat instead of progress.'

George Eliot

. . . and if it ain't broke, break it, on p. 65.

value shared values

Robert Zimmerman felt cut off from the world. He was born in the small town of Hibbing, in Minnesota. It was the middle of nowhere. It was dominated by the largest open-pit iron mine in the world. No one there shared Zimmerman's interest in music, literature and art. No one really understood him. He was operating in isolation. He knew he had to get out and find other creative people so he moved to New York, which was brimming with entrepreneurs, artists, writers and musicians. It was culture central, a focal point for new and exciting ideas. In New York his contemporaries fed him influences, shared discoveries and opened up the world to him – not just in music but in art and poetry. They shared new guitar chords and introduced him to the work of avant-garde poets, which influenced his lyrics. He changed his name to Bob Dylan, which symbolised his rebirth. The atmosphere drove Dylan to explore the boundaries of his talents. He felt more like himself than he ever had before.

A new friend introduced Dylan to the music of Woody Guthrie. The encounter was a revelation for Dylan and showed him a way forward, making him realise that folk music could be a vehicle to communicate the thoughts and ideas that mattered most to him. He was able to create something honest and worthy. He went on to change the way the world perceived singers. Before Dylan, great singers had to have traditional singing skills. He single-handedly ushered in the singer-songwriter era. Suddenly, what you sang about mattered more than how you sang it.

If it wasn't for Sergei Rachmaninov's friends he would have given up early in his career. His powerful Symphony No. 1

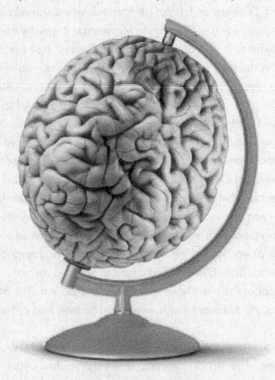

was hated by both critics and the public when it was first performed, and was immediately deemed a failure. The experience had a terrible effect on the young composer, utterly destroying his confidence. Rachmaninov completely lost the urge to compose and wrote nothing for the next three years. His friends set about nursing his fragile confidence back to full fitness; they loved his work and wanted to hear more. His desire to write music returned and he started work on his Piano Concerto No. 2. It was a success and restored the composer's confidence. But in all the years that followed he never attempted to have his first symphony published or performed again. It was a disaster that haunted him until his death.

During World War Two the original score for Symphony No. 1 was discovered by accident and performed again. This time it was an extraordinary success and became one of the most respected compositions of the twentieth century. Rachmaninov, though, did not live to see its belated glory.

Find others who are on your wavelength and share your values. If you're a creative thinker, the chances are that you're challenging the accepted values and practices of your organisation. The problem with organisations is that they don't know what they know. Expertise learned and applied in one area is not used in another.

The most effective way to create a sharing culture is to start to practise it at whatever level you're at. Whether you're high up or low down in an organisation, you can change the culture. Bill Gates called it 'corporate IQ' – the ability of company employees to share knowledge and build on each other's ideas. It's the boss's role to encourage this. 'Power comes not from knowledge kept,' said Gates, 'but from knowledge shared.' But don't sit around waiting for your boss – if your company isn't doing this already, don't wait, start it up for them. Sharing your knowledge creates synergy: you'll get more out than you put in.

'If you have knowledge, let others light their candles in it.'

Margaret Fuller

Feeling competitive rather than collaborative? *Meet some of history's great creative rivals on p. 72.*

light a fire in your mind

Contrast the writer James Joyce with his daughter Lucia. Both were troubled people. Joyce wrote all day, every day. He poured his difficulties into his writing, using his art form as a means of self-analysis and repair. He was his own therapist and became an expert on the workings of his own mind. No doctor could diagnose his problems and cure him better than he could. Writing stabilised his life. Creativity enables us to doctor ourselves. Joyce saw that Lucia, on the other hand, was slipping into madness and valiantly tried to prevent it. He realised her dancing career was not enough to save her, as writing had saved him. He desperately encouraged Lucia to take up illustration and, when that didn't work, writing. She couldn't find an enthusiasm to engross her as Joyce had, and eventually was committed to an asylum.

Joyce commented on Lucia inheriting her challenges from him: 'Whatever spark or gift I possess has been transmitted to Lucia and it has kindled a fire in her brain.' Joyce used the fire in his brain to light up the world of literature. It was a source of inspiration and energy. Lucia's fire had no outlet and burned her up. Joyce saw the opportunity in his difficulties; Lucia saw the difficulty in her opportunities.

Being at the forefront of a discipline is exciting, but it can leave you exposed and vulnerable. Our most astonishing ideas and sense of fulfilment usually spring from our deepest problems. Creativity requires you to study the dark corners of your mind and come to terms with what you find. A creative mind is receptive and highly sensitive and therefore more exposed to deeper lows, but also reaches higher highs. Our most worthwhile achievements come from overcoming our inner demons and putting them to work. The deeper a feeling, the greater the enjoyment in transforming it into something worthwhile. No rain, no rainbow.

'In the depths of winter I finally learned there was in me an invincible summer.'

Albert Camus

More? Be positive about negatives on p. 29.

discover how to discover

Miuccia Prada kept searching, even though she didn't know what she was looking for. She had lived many different lives before discovering fashion. After graduating with a PhD in political science she became a member of the Communist Party and a champion of women's rights. Later, she studied mime for five years at the Piccolo Teatro then performed at venues like La Scala. Eventually these influences were poured into her fashion brand, giving Prada more depth and richer ideals than most fashion houses.

With sales in billions of dollars, Prada became a fashion powerhouse known for understated and classic style. Miuccia Prada was a fashion designer by profession, but she was also an art curator, film producer, fledgling architect, feminist, capitalist and communist.

She created a situation where a great modern designer could be a mogul, a film producer, curator, gallery owner or lightning rod for other creatives who felt connected to her vision of personal transformation. Miuccia's stores don't feel like stores; they're more like cultural spaces where a film, exhibition or performance might take place.

When Miuccia took up fashion, it seemed trivial and shallow in comparison to her leftist feminist ideals. But she saw that fashion could be the first level of emancipation, a cheap way of transforming yourself. 'Fashion is about the way we compose ourselves every day,' Miuccia has said. Her designs shouted, 'Who are you? Dare to find out.' They walk the tightrope of being simultaneously classic and revolutionary.

Miuccia's work and life are a seamless combination. She makes clothes she wants to make, clothes that express her views. Other designers have been touched, more than just by her style, by her thinking and attitude; and they in turn have spread her ideas. Most designers emulate trends, but Prada *is* the trend.

Not everyone is born knowing what he or she wants to do. Many have to discover their passion by trial and error. Along the way they discover things that are useful, even though they don't realise it at the time. The media is full of stories of stars who were 'born' tennis players or 'born' performers; but when you examine their lives more closely it's often the case that their family pushed them into tennis or performing. For most people, discovering what they truly want to do is a gruelling journey, but worth it.

Many people live without direction. Our lives are a path to self-discovery, a journey to ourselves. Van Gogh lived for thirty years before he discovered painting. He sensed he had a purpose, but didn't know what it was. When he took up painting seriously, it was the first time he had found a satisfying outlet for his nervous energy. Painting gave him a deeper understanding of himself.

We have to keep searching. Every important experience adjusts our perspective. Experience is what happens to you. It's what you do with those experiences that matters.

'I may not have gone where I intended to go, but I think I have ended up where I needed to be.'

Douglas Adams

More? Meet another fashion icon who refused to follow the rules on p. 18.
Less? Find out who's to blame for the myth of God-given talent on p. 12.

to stand out, work out
what you stand for

Write a manifesto that sets out your values, as a statement of principles and a call to action. A manifesto is a set of standards to use as a guide – signposts to refer back to when you feel lost. Some of it may be nonsense or contradictory, but it captures the spirit of what drives a creative person. Put down messages to yourself that remind you of what you care about most passionately, then refer to them when you feel you're going off course. Call it a manifesto, a personal mission statement, a vision board or a list – taking the time to identify what you stand for is worthwhile.

Marinetti wrote the first art manifesto of the twentieth century for the Futurists. It wasn't cold and logical like a corporation or political party's manifesto might be, but conveyed intense emotion. It was a random set of statements that declared futurism to be a rejection of the past and a celebration of speed, violence and youth – the things they cared about most.

Other manifesto proclamations: For the Dada movement, poet Tristan Tzara's 1918 Dada Manifesto is a blustering rant:

'DADA DOES NOT MEAN ANYTHING.' André Breton's 1924 *Manifeste du surréalisme* begins, 'We are still living under the reign of logic.' He rails against the supremacy of logic, and sees unleashing the subconscious as the solution.

The designer John Maeda: 'Emotion: More emotions are better than less.' The writer Leo Tolstoy: 'Change nothing in your style of living even if you become ten times richer.' Mark Rothko, Adolph Gottlieb and Barnett Newman: 'This world of imagination is fancy-free and violently opposed to common sense.'

After scouring the manifestos of many companies, the only worthwhile or interesting line I could find was from Apple's: 'We believe in saying no to thousands of projects so that we can really focus on the few that are truly important and meaningful to us.'

Developing a set of principles you believe in and constantly strive to uphold is an invaluable tool. Manifestos are traditionally public declarations, but everyone can also have a personal manifesto. Don't make it a dreary list of worthy intentions drenched in morality. It's a medium through which your present self can correspond with your future self. The only way to stand out is to work out what you stand for.

'Man often becomes what he believes himself to be.'

Mahatma Gandhi

Meet the conservative revolutionaries who knew better than anyone what they stood for on p. 116.

to achieve something, do nothing

The great crime writer Raymond Chandler set aside at least four hours each day to do nothing. He explained his two simple rules: 'A. You don't have to write. B. You can't do anything else. The rest comes of itself.' He didn't force himself to write, but he stopped himself doing anything else. No reading, writing letters, tidying – nothing. He couldn't distract himself. He found that if he was just sitting there, doing nothing, he'd start writing just to pass the time. With nothing to do, his imagination wandered and he'd think up a story. He almost always ended up writing for the full four hours.

Working is a dangerous form of procrastination. Creativity is the most difficult thing the human mind has to tackle. Tidying, cleaning, organising, answering emails, cruising the Internet, doing 'research', reformatting a document, planning meetings, attending meetings, arranging pre-meeting meetings . . . Every other chore seems easier and therefore more alluring.

Do you want a tidy flat and a blank canvas or a messy flat and a completed canvas? Writing this book has caused me to be two years behind on my ironing. We find it hard to pause, or just be still, in our 24/7 culture. Look at people waiting in a queue and you'll see they immediately take out their phones and check their emails and texts. Our hyperactive culture believes it is better to be doing something, even if it's futile or worthless, than doing nothing.

Many writers prefer to write in cafés – J.K. Rowling famously remarked that 'This got me away from the temptations of the Internet. At home, by contrast, there's no end to the useful tasks that I can find to occupy myself.'

Make yourself do nothing. Let your thoughts settle. Sometimes we need to be patient. Instead of searching, things will come to you. The ideas and solutions were within us but we were occupied with other mundane, everyday matters. We were looking in the wrong direction.

Sometimes what we most need to do is the thing we most try to avoid. If you want to do something creative, something original, do nothing.

'It is the job that is never started that takes longest to finish.'

J.R.R. Tolkien

Inspired? *Try working the hours that work for you, and no more, on p. 125 – or achieve the perfect work–life balance on p. 207.*

search high and low

I thought I saw someone vandalising a Jeff Koons sculpture.
It was late evening in New York. The man was wearing what
looked like a surgeon's smock and a fluorescent orange hard
hat. He moved with jerky, manic and intense gestures. I
should have known better, but I couldn't stop myself, I was
compelled to intervene.

The Koons sculpture was *Puppy*, a giant West Highland
terrier made of flowers. *Puppy* combined the two sugary,
sentimental themes of flowers and puppies. Koons stated
that this gaudy monster was a symbol of 'love, warmth,
and happiness'. It towered forty feet above me. Twenty-
three tons of soil covered a steel structure swathed in
70,000 red, orange, white and pink flowering petunias,
begonias and chrysanthemums. It was midway through
construction and the workers had left the site unat-
tended. Close up, I could see the man's darting, frenzied
eyes as he moved the plants around with agitated
movements.

Puppy was a distillation of American culture, big, bright, colourful, popular – and seriously crazy. Art aficionados spent hours pondering its meaning; others simply laughed and enjoyed it. Unlike much contemporary art, it reached out to viewers and they responded. Koons uses kitsch and vulgar sculptures to challenge the accepted aesthetic taste of the 'highbrow'. He constantly stretches and amplifies kitsch and tasteless trash and rubs the noses of exclusive art-world patrons in it. The huge scale of his sculptures makes them unavoidable. He has put gaudy kitsch in the most rarefied museums on the planet. *Puppy* now stands permanently outside the Guggenheim Museum in Bilbao.

The crazy vandal, by the way, of course turned out to be Jeff Koons. A perfectionist, he was working late, attending to details. He was friendly and warm and asked if I'd like to place a few flowers.

Creative thinkers like Koons mock the idea of 'high' and 'low' culture, 'good' or 'bad'. They don't consider an episode of *The Simpsons* to be better or worse than a Shakespeare play. Each has qualities. They see no incompatibility between being tuned in to Jay Z one minute and Mahler the next. If we dismiss 'low' culture we are missing out on a huge area of life. Koons blurred the lines between kitsch and high art. Rock and roll started off firmly in the 'low' category but bands like Pink Floyd completely erased the wall between 'high' and 'low' music.

The terms 'highbrow' and 'lowbrow' come from the populist science of phrenology that boomed in the late nineteenth century. The shape of the skull was used to identify intelligence. A 'high' forehead signified intelligence; a 'low' one meant stupidity. Real science has completely discredited phrenology, but its ideas linger on. You can't think creatively if you have elitist attitudes. Snobbery is a straitjacket.

As well as seeing the value in things that aren't generally valued, creative thinkers also see the value in people who aren't valued. They try to tease out the potential in everyone because they know that no one has a monopoly on creativity.

In 1982 Craig Good was not valued by society. He'd done a variety of jobs and was currently unemployed. He applied for a janitorial and security job in Pixar's General Services department. Scrubbing toilets was the main task. 'If you want to learn a lot about a company,' Good said, 'being a janitor is a pretty good way to do it.' Pixar at that point was still a department within Lucasfilm. They offered an after-work programming course to any company employees. Good attended, and was soon moved to the company's computer division.

Good eventually became a camera artist at Pixar, a job he did for thirty years. He was famous for his work on *Toy Story*, *Finding Nemo* and *Monsters, Inc*. Good's career was proof that Pixar valued all employees for their potential, no matter what their position.

'One of the characteristics that made Pixar, and is very rare and important, is that the corporate culture recognised that contributions can come from everybody, anybody,' Pam Kerwin, Pixar's vice-president, has said. Pixar screens each film numerous times for everyone in the company while it is in production, and invites anyone to make suggestions. It has the effect of making everyone feel valued. To develop a strong creative workplace, people need to feel comfortable in expressing their ideas. Many Pixar employees have left to start businesses of their own and transferred that attitude to create new revolutionary products and vigorous teams. Many have gone into non-art and design areas such as manufacturing, service industries and retail; they have proved that creative thinking will benefit any company.

Creative thinkers put aside the value judgements that affect the rest of society. They don't assume that because everyone thinks something is worthless, it actually is worthless. They are able to see things clearly and assess them according to their own values.

'Our attitudes control our lives. Attitudes are a secret power working twenty-four hours a day, for good or bad. It is of paramount importance that we know how to harness and control this great force.'

Irving Berlin

Inspired to suspend judgement? *Listen out for the sweetest sound of all on p. 146.*

get into credit

There was an extraordinary outburst of creativity in Florence during the early fourteen hundreds. Great artists sprang up like flowers. Donatello, Ghiberti and Masaccio created a huge number of art history's greatest masterpieces. Was it caused by a freak mutation in the gene responsible for creativity?

No, it was money. Florence was the richest city in Europe due to trading and manufacture. There were a dozen major bankers, including the Medici, earning fortunes in interest from money lent to foreign countries. The Medici spent astronomical sums of money on the architects and artists who built and decorated Florence. Wealthy patrons commissioned all the great artworks. Artists flocked to Florence like bees to a honeypot. The seeds of the Renaissance were planted and bloomed, creating civilisation as we know it.

Creativity flourishes where there is money. Money is not the enemy of creative thinkers but the friend; not a problem but an opportunity. The creative mind needs to focus on creativity; financial worries are at best a distraction and at worst a crippling weight. Research shows that the size of Van Gogh's canvases fluctuated in proportion to his finances. Lack of money literally shrank his paintings. Over 5,000 American artists and writers, among them Mark Rothko, Jackson Pollock, Ben Shahn and Jack Kerouac, benefitted from the American government pouring money into the Federal Art Project – a Scheme to promote American culture during World War Two. Artists, writers and musicians were financed for two years, which gave them the time and space to develop, to find their voices. The flowering of Young British Artists in London in the nineteen-eighties was largely due to Charles Saatchi's generous development of his art collection – in turn financed by the boom in advertising revenues. Holland was the richest nation in seventeenth-century Europe and saw the golden age of Dutch painting, with Frans Hals, Vermeer, Jan Steen and Rembrandt. The history of art is inseparable from the history of money.

There are those who work to earn money, and those who work because their work is what they love to do. One of the functions of the wealthy is to finance creativity. With their wealth they buy paintings, cars, houses, yachts, theatre tickets, music – all produced by creative people. They finance the creative and enable them to continue their work.

Artists are usually coy about discussing money because it is uncool. But wealth is a facilitator. It makes things possible. It is fuel for creativity. 'When I hear the word "culture" I bring out my chequebook,' joked a character in the Jean-Luc Godard film *Contempt*. Worrying about money is wasted time and effort. I've never met a successful writer, artist or creative person who wasn't good at managing, or had hired someone to manage, their finances.

'Money is better than poverty, if only for financial reasons.'

Woody Allen

Feeling the pinch? Learn how to prosper in a recession on p. 253.

mine your mind

Many entrepreneurs' best ideas have come to them in their dreams. Elias Howe is credited with inventing the modern sewing machine, which has been remarkably successful due to its innovation of putting the eye of the needle at the point.

Howe's family members explained how he came up with the idea. In his first attempts he put the eye of the needle at the conventional end but it didn't work. Then one night he had a dream in which he was ordered to build a sewing machine by a cruel king in a strange country. The king gave him twenty-four hours or he'd be executed. He struggled with the needle's eye but, just as in real life, he couldn't make it work. He was taken out to be executed and noticed the soldiers had spears that were pierced near the point. The solution presented itself. The inventor begged for more time. At that point he woke up. It was four in the morning. He jumped out of bed, ran to his workshop and created a needle with an eye at the point.

In Sigmund Freud's book *On Creativity and the Unconscious* he analysed the creative mind. Freud believed that as children we used play to express our creativity and imagination. We shared our feelings freely with others and enacted our fantasies unselfconsciously. As adults we become responsible and serious and substitute imaginative play with daydreaming. Dreams are a valuable road into ideas and practical solutions.

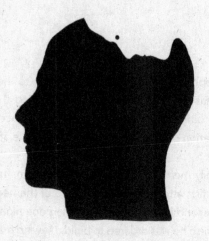

When an employee is standing at the office water cooler and daydreaming, that's probably the most important thing they've done all day. Many creative people have dreamed their products or services. The subconscious is a recognised source of creativity and inspiration; it releases us from the confines of our logical, practical mind. Great creative thinkers appreciate that looking deep into the workings of their minds reveals the unique and unexpected – but we have to mine for them. Our conscious minds are too busy and preoccupied with day-to-day tasks to notice our great ideas.

When our conscious mind is switched off – because we are driving, taking a shower or whatever – ideas suddenly bubble up to the surface. When we are not trying to think, the door to the cage opens and our minds fly off in unpredictable directions and often land on the solution unexpectedly. Salvador Dalí had dreamed about a hand with hundreds of ants crawling over it. The film director Luis Buñuel dreamed of a cloud cutting through the moon like a razor blade slicing through an eye. They put the two together in a film called *Un Chien Andalou* and created one of cinema's most memorable moments. Richard Wagner dreamed the prelude to *Das Rheingold*. Lewis Carroll's *Alice's Adventures in Wonderland* is a journey into his subconscious.

During sleep your mind dips into unconsciousness. Your subconscious continues to ponder on issues or problems your conscious mind has been working on, even when you're not aware of it. The benefit is that in the subconscious, rationality does not censor unusual or irrational ideas. Ideas that would be rejected by the logical mind as too weird are given a chance to grow. Your conscious mind follows whatever rules you've learned; your thoughts are linear and trapped on familiar and predictable lines. In the subconscious mind, bizarre ideas can be explored and might lead to special solutions.

We all daydream. It is something that happens to us naturally and can't be avoided. Our mind wanders everywhere. You need to take advantage of the ideas and concepts you could find when exploring your subconscious. Try putting aside logical and practical thoughts and dig a little deeper for a while. The creative ideas you're searching for are swimming beneath the surface of your mind. You need to find ways to help them break the surface. The more you dive, the more you'll discover.

'The world needs dreamers and the world needs doers. But above all, the world needs dreamers who do.'

Sarah Ban Breathnach

Feeling dreamy? *Follow Hans Christian Andersen and go out of your mind on p. 260.*
Already had your good idea? *Bring it to life on p. 94.*

look forward to disappointment

When Beethoven was young he struggled to earn a living as a musician, to get married and lead a normal life. When he finally achieved success, in his late twenties, he began to lose his hearing. It was his lowest point. He sank into a deep depression. In a letter he declares: 'The most beautiful years of my life must pass without accomplishing the promise of my talent and powers.' Six months later, Beethoven decided 'No! I cannot endure it. I will take Fate by the throat; it shall not wholly overcome me.' Thus began his rise to the summit of his achievements.

Beethoven overcame the obstacle of his total deafness and transformed it into a positive force. He found a way to compose achingly beautiful music. Adversity introduced him to himself. He had to come to terms with his anger and frustration. His music conveys this self-reflection and self-awareness; he used his compositions to come to a greater understanding of himself. Beethoven's music was a healing force for himself, and so in turn it helps us heal our wounds.

Beethoven's works are autobiographical and explore his

turbulent life. They speak to us in a universal and positive way. The stunning piano sonata Opus 110 is about overcoming deafness. Beethoven reassures us that when everything falls apart we have the *Moonlight Sonata*. If you are thinking massive thoughts there is the Ninth Symphony. There is the struggle and triumph of the Fifth Symphony and the heroic Eroica Symphony. Music, and in particular the piano, was his voice, and through it he tells us his autobiography. Beethoven reassures us that he overcame his obstacles and so can we.

When you are at your lowest, when everything that could go wrong has gone wrong, see it as the best place to begin. We learn more from disappointments than from successes. Every obstacle we overcome strengthens our confidence to overcome others. When we respond constructively to big crises it brings out our inner strength. Pain may be inevitable, we'll all experience loss and heartbreak; but great creative people like Beethoven show us that suffering is optional.

There is a time to accept the cards you've been dealt and a time to fight against them. Things always seem to turn out best for those who make the best out of the way things turn out. Beethoven overcame the seemingly insurmountable obstacle of deafness and refused to allow it to destroy him. A creative person always has their ideas, ambitions, passions and memories to support them.

'All misfortune is but a stepping stone to fortune.'

Henry David Thoreau

Feeling restricted? *Turn it to your advantage on p. 263.*

think with your feelings

The teacher handed out toothpicks and semi-dried peas and asked the class to make model buildings. The children formed cubes because that's what they were used to seeing in the streets. A boy with severely bad eyesight, however, had only touch to rely on and discovered that the triangle (or tetrahedron) felt far more solid and stable than fragile squares. He quickly constructed complicated latticeworks. Due to the triangle's strength as a shape, his structures were much bigger and more elegant than his classmates'. The teacher was astonished and called the other children over to see the unique construction. The boy was surprised at their surprise – it had seemed natural to him. His bad eyesight prevented him from seeing the box-like lines of the houses, windows and door frames we are all surrounded by, so he had used touch, and achieved better results.

Two decades later, the boy had become a man and developed his childhood structure into the beautiful and graceful geodesic dome. Based on the simplest of geometric shapes, this is an incredibly strong structure that has no internal supports and can create gigantic spaces. It's easily constructed and transported and very economical. There are now hundreds of thousands all over the world. The boy was Buckminster Fuller, and he went on to become a ground-breaking American architect, designer and inventor. The incident when Fuller was at kindergarten illustrates the benefits of perceiving the world differently. His vision was – literally – radically different to everyone else's.

We think that thinking is the solution. We are focused on thinking our way out of a problem, thinking our way around this and thinking our way through that. We use think tanks and brainstorming. Our culture places such a huge emphasis on thinking that we neglect our senses. Thinking can be a trap. Most of our ideas and knowledge have been inherited from our culture, schools and parents. We are taught how to think and what to think, but any creative person will tell you that thinking only gets you so far. Thinking is essential, but we use it to the detriment of other perceptions.

Many creative people find that to be an authentic version of themselves they have to think with their senses. Our minds play tricks on us but our feelings are trustworthy. We have been taught to choose the respectable, socially acceptable and well-trodden path that everyone else walks down. Instead, choose the path that feels right to you.

'Better to be without logic than without feeling.'

Charlotte Brontë

Still overthinking? Try contradicting yourself on p. 220

bring chaos to order

The Guggenheim Museum in Bilbao, Spain is full of surprises. The outside walls are cloaked in titanium tiles that create a weightless and iridescent feel. The fixing clips make a shallow dent in each thin tile that gives the surface a rippling and ethereal appearance reminiscent of fish scales. Inside, the complex shapes that whirl above the soaring, 150-foot-high atrium are a revelation. To the side, light is diffused through glass slashes in the teetering walls, casting perpetually changing, astonishing shadows. The building is like a car crash – that is meant as a compliment. The distorted and dislocated areas create dynamic and unexpected clashes. Metal crashes into stone, man-made smashes into natural and flowing forms slice into rigid angular forms. The Guggenheim is a great advert for the benefits of chaos over order. Simply walking through it is exciting and energising.

Frank Gehry is one of architecture's great visionaries. Inventive and irreverent, his twisted forms break the conventions of building design. Gehry's playful and sensual structures always stir up controversy. Much of his work falls within the style of deconstructivism, characterised by unpredictability, chaos and fragmentation. The Guggenheim was an audacious design that shook architecture to its core. It opened in 1997 and was acclaimed as the greatest and most magnificent building of its time. The Guggenheim was a dramatic success and its cultural and economic impact on the formerly unknown Spanish city was immense.

The success of the Guggenheim was due to Gehry's insistence that the vision of the architect should be dominant throughout the construction process. Artistic vision is usually put to one side during the construction of a building and practicality is dominant. With the Guggenheim there was no compromise. The construction industry puts pressure on architects to provide extensive blueprints of a building; Gehry ignored that convention. The precision and detail of practical drawings destroys creativity. The architect has to think practically. Practical thinking produces something predictable and conventional. Contractors hired to build the Guggenheim were simply given Gehry's small model. They had to work out the measurements from the architect's model. This resulted in inaccuracies – which Gehry liked. Not having detailed plans made the construction process chaotic. The contractors had to work things out for themselves and devise completely new construction techniques. That is why the Guggenheim is such a wonderful environment, with chaotic twists and turns that keep you continually surprised and delighted.

Why, then, is our culture so obsessed with order? Many urban buildings from the last sixty years were built to the strict rules of the austere Bauhaus movement, with its emphasis on rationality and functionality. We're surrounded by geometric, inhuman cities of right-angled boxes and grids. These city-scapes lead people into behaving like machines, moving from box-like buildings into box-like rooms where they tidy their belongings into boxes. Our offices and studios affect how we behave. This orthodoxy of orderliness crushes creative spirits.

Orderly surroundings force us to think in an orderly way. Creative thinking is unconventional thinking and it flourishes in a disorderly environment. Research in 2013 by Vohs, Redden and Rahinel of the University of Minnesota's Carlson School of Management found that participants assigned to a disorderly room produced more creative solutions than those assigned to a neat and tidy room.

What's true of a Spanish architectural masterpiece is also true of our workplace. It flies in the face of conventional wisdom, but a chaotic office or studio is more productive. Chaotic organisations are more creative than well-organised ones. Distrust the idea that we should strive for order. Order restricts and limits us.

'If a cluttered desk is a sign of a cluttered mind, of what, then, is an empty desk a sign?'

Albert Einstein

Inspired? Try improvising your way out of a problem on p. 239.
Uninspired? Meet a slightly more methodical creative on p. 235.

take what you need

A student at Stanford University discovered the short stories of John Cheever. He decided to type them out word for word, page for page. He stepped into Cheever's shoes and felt what it was like to have 'written' them. Rather like da Vinci dissecting a heart to try to understand how it worked, the student was trying to get inside Cheever's mind. He went on to become the prolific fiction writer Ethan Canin; there have been four Hollywood films based on his stories. 'It's interesting because you learn things,' Canin explained. 'Something simple about Cheever is that his paragraphs are much longer than yours would have been. His sentences are longer. He pushes everything further than I would have pushed them.' From that 'pushing further' Canin learned to be more extreme in his writing. He learned from Cheever's technique, then he learned from Cheever's mind – how he thought about things. Canin failed to emulate him accurately, though. Humans are not photocopy machines. Where he failed to copy Cheever accurately was where he began to be original. That's where he was different. It was this difference he magnified. You can borrow flour, but you have to bake your own bread.

Copying as an exercise is not the same as plagiarism. Plagiarism would be if you signed a painting someone else has done, or otherwise pretended you did someone else's work. Everyone has influences. The reason that great artists cluster together geographically is so that they can learn from each other. Jacques Lipchitz explains, 'I remember one day when Juan Gris told me about a bunch of grapes he had seen in a painting by Picasso. The next day these grapes appeared in a painting by Gris, this time in a bowl; and the day after, the bowl appeared in a painting by Picasso.'

Many people have the urge to create, but nothing to say. They have no ideas and even if they did, they wouldn't know how to express them. So to get the ball rolling, they copy other creative people's ideas. Why not? It's a starting point. Copying is misunderstood by people who are not creative. A lot of our behaviour comes from observing and emulating others, not least fundamental abilities like walking and talking. Later, we practise what the psychologist Albert Bandura refers to as 'modelling'. We are more likely to smoke if our friends smoke, more likely to overeat if our friends overeat. You become those you imitate. So choose carefully which creative thinkers you emulate.

One of the secrets to being creative is to analyse and gain an understanding of the genius of others, then rework it for your own purposes. Rembrandt was an apprentice but he went on to produce entirely original paintings. He learned from the masters, but then his unique vision emerged. When you see a piece of work you admire, dissect it scientifically and discover exactly what makes it great. Is it the style? The concept? The creator's personality? You need to unashamedly take ideas and techniques from anywhere.

'Chance favours the connected mind.'

Steven Johnson

Hungry to cross-pollinate? Try p. 246. **Prefer to strive for something completely original?** Surprise yourself with your own story on p. 138.

remake, then remake the remake

The composer and lyricist Stephen Sondheim had a flop on his hands. When the Broadway production of his musical *Merrily We Roll Along* opened, the critics savaged it and it ran for only sixteen performances. Audiences were confused and couldn't follow the story. It was a shock for him; he has written many great musicals, including *West Side Story*, and won Academy Awards, Grammys; you name a theatre award and he's won it. So how did he deal with a flop?

Sondheim reworked *Merrily We Roll Along*, again and again. Over the years the musical has been restaged with numerous songs discarded and replaced with new versions. Each time it was performed he revised it by adding a new song. Sondheim believed in the musical, sure of his ability, sure of his original idea but able to question and to deconstruct the parts that didn't work for audiences. Eventually it showed in London and then back on Broadway to ecstatic reviews, decades after its first disastrous appearance.

The first spark of inspiration always needs reworking and revision. Ernest Hemingway explained, 'I rewrote the ending to Farewell to Arms, the last page of it, thirty-nine times before I was satisfied.' That means he discarded thirty-eight chapters. He constantly took an axe to his work and rebuilt it. The creative enjoy the revision process – carving away excess words, clay or notes until the rhythm and phrasing of their work purrs like a well-tuned engine. Many ask for help with their revision process. T.S. Eliot enlisted Ezra Pound to give him extensive feedback on his most important poem, The Waste Land. In the original manuscript Pound has scribbled numerous comments such as 'verse not interesting enough'. Without Pound's help it would never have become a classic.

Many early versions of a work need to be discarded before it can be rendered into a coherent form. When a printing deadline approached, J.R.R. Tolkien, author of The Lord of the Rings, intensively revised, reconsidered and polished his manuscript. Tolkien rewrote so thoroughly that many new ideas sprang from him and the publisher, expecting a completed text, instead often received the first draft of a completely new work. D.H. Lawrence rewrote Lady Chatterley's Lover from start to finish three times before it was ready to publish. Similarly, Picasso's greatest masterpiece, the huge oil painting Guernica, has been presented as a bolt from the blue, a flash of inspiration. The myth is that Picasso heard of the bombing of the small town of Guernica during the Spanish Civil War and painted an instinctive response: a visual account of the devastating and chaotic impact of war on both men and women, specifically on civilian life and communities. What is less well known is that Picasso produced forty-five preliminary sketches for *Guernica* before he even began painting. Archive photos of the painting in progress reveal numerous layers of adjustments and radical changes; the final product took weeks to paint.

Artists, writers and other creative people often speak of finding what they have to say in the process of trying to say it. First drafts of composers', writers' and artists' work are truly revealing because they often expose that seismic alterations have been made. Be prepared to constantly rethink and revise.

'You might not write well every day, but you can always edit a bad page. You can't edit a blank page.'

Jodi Picoult

More? Meet a quartet that exemplifies the merits of working hard to make it look easy on p. 25.
Less? Cut it out on p. 60.

be curious about curiosity

Eric Blair deliberately got himself arrested so that he could spend Christmas in prison. He was curious to see what it would be like. Unfortunately the authorities didn't consider his disorderly behaviour serious enough and released him. Blair was fascinated by how people at the opposite end of the social spectrum lived. He was born into an elite, wealthy, upper-class family and educated at Eton. Suddenly he began dressing in ragged clothes and shoes and lived rough on the streets of London and Paris with beggars and the homeless. Reading about poverty was not enough for him; he wanted to experience it for himself. He didn't carry spare money for emergencies or wear layers of clothes for protection against the freezing conditions. He wanted the authentic feel of hunger, cold and hopelessness.

Blair's experiences were recorded in the book *Down and Out in Paris and London*, vivid experiences of the places and characters he found living on the margins. Although he describes the squalor and degradation in detail, the result is fascinating and revealing. He exposes extraordinary life stories as well as the resourcefulness and resilience of people discarded by society. He challenged his prejudices, cultivated his curiosity and discovered years' worth of inspiration for writing and novels. He changed his name to George Orwell so that his parents and friends wouldn't be embarrassed by his exploits and went on to write some of the twentieth century's classic novels, including *1984* and *Animal Farm*.

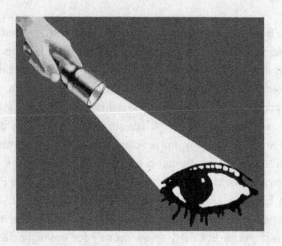

The future belongs to the curious. Curiosity makes us come alive; it fills us with wonder and the urge to search. We discover hidden worlds. Our imaginations are ignited. Curiosity is the engine of achievement. It's what drives us to keep questioning, keep discovering and continue to break new ground. As Einstein famously said, 'I have no special talents. I am only passionately curious.'

Curious people search for the reality behind the façade, for what's truly going on behind the scenes. They ask difficult questions. Albert Einstein explained further, 'The important thing is not to stop questioning. Curiosity has its own reason for existing. One cannot help but be in awe when he contemplates the mysteries of eternity, of life, of the marvellous structure of reality. It is enough if one tries merely to comprehend a little of this mystery every day.' Researching a subject is important but the creative research creatively. We can decide to be curious. We can recognise the need for it and then nurture it. Curiosity refreshes stale viewpoints and creates new perspectives.

'The cure for boredom is curiosity. There is no cure for curiosity.'

Dorothy Parker

Curiosity not sated? Try projecting yourself into the future on p. 256.

become anonymous

When J.K. Rowling had become the world's highest-selling author, she stunned the book world by revealing that The Cuckoo's Calling was her work, written under the pseudonym Robert Galbraith. Rowling said, 'I had hoped to keep this secret a little longer, because being Robert Galbraith has been such a liberating experience.' Agatha Christie wrote sixty-six successful detective novels under her own name. She also wrote six romance novels under the name Mary Westmacott. Christie wanted to explore another genre without the baggage of her reputation pulling her down. Many novelists want to experiment with new genres. John Banville achieved recognition as a serious writer by winning the Man Booker prize in 2005, but also writes crime novels as Benjamin Black to mask his identity. Julian Barnes, another Man Booker-winning author, writes thrillers as Dan Kavanagh. A pseudonym gave them all the freedom to write without the shackles of their reputations, and an opportunity to explore genres that are not generally taken seriously.

Robert Towne is a legendary Hollywood scriptwriter. He worked behind the scenes on classics such as *Bonnie and Clyde* and *The Godfather*, for which he didn't demand any credit. He mentored Jeremy Larner, who won an Oscar for writing *The Candidate*. 'I couldn't have written it without him,' said Larner. Sometimes Towne was hired to write a script for which he knew he'd get the credit; weeks and months would go by without a script materialising. If Towne was working anonymously he worked freely and quickly. If he knew he was going to get the credit for a script, he suffered from writer's block. He kept rewriting and rewriting but the script didn't ever reach a conclusion. Eventually he would be given a deadline. He wouldn't keep to it and was often dropped from the project. After working for years on a film called *Greystoke: The Legend of Tarzan, Lord of the Apes*, Towne became disillusioned and gave the credit for the script to his dog, P.H. Vazak. Vazak was the first dog nominated for an Academy Award for screenwriting.

Sometimes it's good to put your ego in a box under the bed. There is freedom in being nobody. We live in a culture where everyone is obsessed with getting credit for every little thing they do. Many writers have written books using pseudonyms to give themselves the freedom to experiment and make mistakes. They don't want the credit for writing them – they simply want to enjoy writing.

If we are not accountable for something, we work with freedom. We experiment in a way we would not normally have the nerve to. Sometimes our egos get in the way and tie us up in knots. Working in anonymity will free you of others' expectations but, most importantly, free you of your own expectations.

'It's that anonymous person who meanders through the streets and feels what's happening there, feels the pulse of the people, who's able to create.'

Cyndi Lauper

Ego still bothering you? *Get out of yourself on p. 260, or remind yourself of the pleasures of obscurity on p. 155.*

achieve the perfect work–life balance

The way to achieve the perfect work–life balance is to not do any work. If your work and life are in separate compartments, something's gone wrong. Great painters, poets, dancers, artists, entrepreneurs and creative people choose a lifestyle and then work out what they have to do to make a living within that way of life. They choose a fulfilling way of life rather than fulfilling society's expectations. When they are writing, painting, dancing or whatever, they are doing what makes them truly and authentically themselves and would not want to be doing anything else.

Hunter S. Thompson, spokesman for the beat generation, wanted to spend his life writing, so he set about earning his living through journalism and writing novels such as *Fear and Loathing in Las Vegas*. Thompson was never rich, but he was never poor either and he lived the lifestyle that suited him. He fulfilled his potential as a writer. A ceremony was held for him after he died in which his ashes were fired from a cannon. He literally went out with a bang.

Hunter S. Thompson jotted down this advice to a friend: 'As I see it then, the formula runs something like this: a man must choose a path that will let his abilities function at maximum efficiency toward the gratification of his desires.' Thompson continues, 'In short, he has not dedicated his life to reaching a pre-defined goal, but he has rather chosen a way of life he knows he will enjoy.' Thompson achieved these ambitions. He sometimes had to scratch out a living through journalism, but he was writing what he believed and that was what mattered most.

The creative person's work and life are one, inseparable. They are their work. There is no 'balance' because they are bound together. Once your life and work head down separate paths you are destined for a schizophrenic lifestyle. If you'd rather go on holiday than go to work – you need to change your life, now.

'If you're interested in "balancing" work and pleasure, stop trying to balance them. Instead make your work more pleasurable.'

Donald Trump

Inspired? Try changing your body clock at the same time on p. 125.

make what you say unforgettable

The celebrated physiologist Giles Brindley created an original way to convey his ideas. The audience will never forget his lecture at the American Urological Association meeting in Las Vegas in 1983. It made an impact that would have taken conventional speakers years to achieve. The *New York Times* declared Brindley's spectacle the start of a 'second sexual revolution'. Brindley's lecture was cited as the catalyst for the revolution that followed and the introduction of Viagra a decade later.

Brindley's talk took place just before a formal dinner reception, to an audience of rather pompous doctors and their wives dressed in dinner suits and evening gowns. Brindley explained his theory: that it was possible to inject chemicals into the penis to cause an erection. At the time very little was known about erectile physiology. Viagra, and the days when politicians and soccer legends spoke candidly about their struggles with erectile dysfunction, were years away.

In the absence of suitable animal models, Brindley had experimented on himself. He showed images of his own penis in various states of tumescence – much to the audience's surprise. He explained that it was such an effective method that a single dose made an impotent man stay hard for hours.

Brindley was concerned that sceptics might question whether erotic stimulation had played a part in achieving

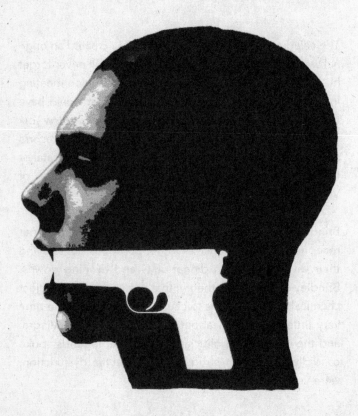

the results. The professor wanted to make his case in the most convincing way possible, so he had injected himself shortly before the talk. He pointed out that no one would find the experience of giving a lecture to a large audience erotically stimulating, then dropped his trousers to reveal his clearly erect penis. There was not a sound in the room. Everyone had stopped breathing. Brindley then said, 'I'd like to give some of the audience the opportunity to confirm the degree of tumescence.' He shuffled to the first row of the horrified audience. Women in the front rows threw their arms up in the air and screamed loudly. The screams seemed to shock Professor Brindley (who later received a knighthood for his bioengineering research) and he rapidly pulled up his trousers, returned to the podium and terminated the lecture. The crowd dispersed in a state of stunned silence.

The impact of Brindley's lecture changed the course of men's health for ever. It was a revolutionary concept. He proved that an erection could happen without any emotional or erotic arousal; that it could be achieved in a purely physical way. More importantly, he found a creative way to make an impact on the medical world.

An original thinker is a scout on new horizons, a font of inspiration. They find a way to communicate an idea that makes it impossible to forget. They are creative in the way they get their message across. If you have an interesting idea, it's important that people remember it. The people who have changed our thinking are the ones who speak and write from the heart with the courage to be simply who they are. You have the courage to head towards a new frontier without a map.

> *'Once something is memorable, it's living and you're using it. That to me is the foundation of a creative society.'*

Yo-Yo Ma

More? Learn how to be as annoying as Jonathan Swift on p. 244.
Less? See the downside of nudity during public speaking on p. 50.

don't experiment, *be* an experiment

The Beatles became the most influential cultural force of their era by following a principle: constant experimentation. They searched for new methods to make music, consistently explored new musical territory with each album, and when they describe how they worked in the recording studio, it sounds more like a sound laboratory. More fundamentally, they continually reinvented their music by injecting it with fresh influences. Paul McCartney explained their recording philosophy: 'We would say, "Try it. Just try it for us. If it sounds crappy, OK, we'll lose it. But it might just sound good." We were always pushing ahead: louder, further, longer, more, different.' They experimented with mixing several genres together. They were the first rock band to use feedback 'I Feel Fine', the sitar and Indian music on *Revolver*, a string quartet on 'Yesterday'. The Beatles loved technology: they used artificial double tracking, close miking of acoustic instruments, sampling, direct injection, synchronising tape machines and playing tapes backwards. All these experiments added the multiple dimensions to their work that makes it so deeply layered.

The reason why Lennon and McCartney are the most successful musical collaboration in history is because they constantly played around with ways to improve each other's songs. Occasionally two incomplete songs that each had produced individually would be added together to create a complete song ('A Day in the Life', for example). Sometimes one of the two added a middle eight to the other's verse and chorus. Lennon called it 'Writing eyeball to eyeball'. It created an atmosphere where they felt free to add all kinds of experimental ideas to each other's songs. When you listen to tapes of them in the studio they are always adding jokes, outrageous lyrics and strange sounds to each other's basic song.

The key to thinking experimentally is to allow the mind to contemplate outrageous ideas. It requires enormous effort.

Apply judgements about practicality, legality and ethics only at the end. We are taught by our culture to dismiss novel and seemingly ridiculous ideas at the outset to save time, and to think logically. We have to suppress that urge; we could all do it naturally when we were young, but we seem to lose it as we get older.

It's more interesting to be experimental and fail than play safe and succeed. When I was a student at the Royal College of Art, the student working next to me found an old painting on a scrap of paper at the back of a drawer. He liked parts of it, so he cut it up into pieces and then stuck them down in a new arrangement that was much more interesting than the original. I looked closely at it. I could see fragments of writing scattered across the composition. I pointed out that the fragments were the signature of a previous student, 'David Hockney'. I have never seen anyone go so white. The student had transformed an old painting into something better, but reduced its value from tens of thousands of pounds to nothing. The moral of the story? Sometimes there's a downside to experimentation: not all experiments are successful. To get into the experimental mindset, you have to accept that there will be a lot of fruitless attempts, even disasters. There is no way of knowing what will work and what won't, but every failed experiment will teach you something new.

We are all confronted by problems, but an experimental approach can lead to unique and original solutions. Creative thinkers imagine their office, studio or workplace as a place to experiment, a laboratory. Creative organisations practise constant experimentation to keep their thinking fresh.

It's in the nature of experiments that they are sometimes unsuccessful. If you're trying out new things, they may not work. But if things are running too smoothly, it is a sign that you're not experimenting enough.

'I have always been more interested in experiment than in accomplishment.'

Orson Welles

Agree? Find something that's working and break it on p. 65.

Disagree? Find something that doesn't need improving and improve it on p. 158.

stop missing opportunities

How many opportunities have you missed? I've lost count of the number of people I know who have been given one and didn't take it. They were blasé. They assumed another would come along, then another and another. But it didn't. They had one chance, and they let it pass them by. In retrospect, they bitterly regret it. Opportunities are often rare and fleeting.

The great Hollywood actor, director and producer Warren Beatty was nominated for fifteen Academy Awards during his career, and once won the Best Director Award. His most famous acting role was as Clyde Barrow in *Bonnie and Clyde*. In 1964 he wanted to put together a film he could star in. His idea became *What's New Pussycat?* It was a comedy about a notorious womaniser who wanted to be faithful to his girlfriend but was continually tempted by women who kept falling in love with him.

Beatty found a producer and they set to work on the script. They soon realised they needed someone to write good jokes. At a club in New York called The Bitter End they saw a young comic called Woody Allen doing stand-up. He was funny, so they offered him $30,000 a week to add a few jokes to the script. Allen tried to get $40,000 a week. 'No' was the response. Allen said he'd do it for $30,000 if he could also have a small cameo role. They agreed.

Allen went to work. As draft followed draft, Beatty noticed that his role was getting slighter as the unknown Allen's got bigger. Allen continued to expand his character as Beatty's shrank smaller and smaller. Eventually Beatty angrily stormed away from the project. *What's New Pussycat?* went on to be a big success. From that moment on, Allen was a significant Hollywood A-lister and made sure he was always in total control of his work. He made the most of his opportunity. He might never have got another one. It was a small opportunity but he made it big. He went on to greater and greater film projects.

I've known many artists who were offered a one-person exhibition – their big chance! – but argued with the gallery owner about some small contractual detail and the deal fell through. They were never offered another exhibition. I've known writers who wanted a slightly bigger royalty than the publisher was offering. They rejected it, but it turned out to be the only book deal they were ever offered. It was their big break. They assumed there would be more, but there weren't. They vanish into oblivion. If you're a nobody, it's not a good idea to be a difficult nobody. When you're a somebody, you can be a difficult somebody. Even then, it's probably not wise.

When you're given a break, take it and see where it leads, even if you have no idea how you'll make it work. Say 'yes', then work out how to bring it off. Rise to the occasion when an occasion arises.

'One secret of success in life is for a man to be ready for his opportunity when it comes.'

Benjamin Disraeli

Can't see any opportunities worth taking? *Create your own on p. 22, or hold out for a recession on p. 253.*

contradict yourself more often

'One is fruitful only at the cost of being rich in contradictions,' said Friedrich Nietzsche. Research into creative
thinkers has revealed that they have personalities full of
contradictions. Eminent psychologist Mihaly Csikszentmihalyi
has discovered that creative people 'contain contradictory
extremes; instead of being an individual, each of them is a
multitude.'

The English painter Francis Bacon was a fascinating example
of how conflicting personality traits are essential to produce
great art. Bacon was a giant of twentieth-century art who
captured the anxieties and frenetic energy of the century
with brutality and tenderness. His violent paintings are
revered and hated in equal measure.

In many ways Bacon's paintings are indecisive. They are
portraits, but the people in them are often unrecognisable.
They lurch from abstract areas to figurative passages. They
are often titled 'studies' because Bacon was unable to
decide whether or not they were finished.

Psychologists use extroversion and introversion as the most stable personality traits with which to measure people. They can't do this with creative individuals because they exhibit both traits simultaneously, tending to be both extroverted and introverted, sometimes the centre of attention, sometimes observers on the fringes. Again, Bacon exemplified this paradox. He frequented the Colony Room, a private members' drinking club in London's Soho that was a magnet for the capital's aspiring creatives. Out with friends, I sometimes found myself in that glorious hellhole. Bacon was usually centre stage, in the thick of the party, but only after he'd spent countless long, solitary hours in his studio. He frequently switched from extroversion to introversion.

Bacon exhibited another classic contradiction of creative thinkers: he was simultaneously rebellious and conservative. He was deeply immersed in the traditions and history of painting; he used oil on canvas, painted mainly portraits and placed his paintings in large gold frames. Yet he challenged traditions. He painted on the 'wrong', unprimed side of the canvas, he applied the paint with dustbin lids and rags rather than brushes and his subject matter was shocking and outrageous.

It's impossible to be creative without having a deep understanding of an area of culture, but a creative person has to be rebellious and iconoclastic to break away from the safety of tradition and make something different. As Georges Bataille asserted, 'I believe that truth has only one face: that of a violent contradiction.'

Francis Bacon was intensely passionate about his work, yet at the same time highly objective about it. He was capable of being totally immersed in a painting for hours and days, then suddenly switching to being objective and detached to a point where he'd slash and destroy a substandard painting with a knife. Without passion, we soon abandon a difficult task. Yet without objectivity we can't assess our work.

Bacon's personality contained numerous contradictions; among them, he was playful but highly disciplined and humble yet arrogant. His admiration of Rembrandt and Van Gogh ensured that he could put his own contribution modestly in perspective. Yet he would belittle and humiliate painters he considered third rate.

His paintings are great art because they reflect the contradictions of his mind. He painted savagely gashed human flesh – with sensitivity. A painstakingly worked area of paint was then attacked by a wildly thrown splash. His brushwork was brutal yet tender. Most of his works contain an area of jet black against pure white. These contrasts create tension and excitement. It's the contradictions within his mind, and therefore within the paintings, that make them great art.

Although they can be perplexing and frustrating to others, contradictions are an inextricable element of creativity. There is pressure in our culture to make clear what you stand for, to make a decision and stick to it. It's practically a criminal offence to change your mind. The result is rigid thinking. What is true of the individual is also true of organisations. 'It is really dangerous if everyone in a company starts thinking the same way,' Michael Dell, chairman and CEO of Dell Inc., has said. He encourages his employees to attack problems from different perspectives. The creative mind has to contain multiple perspectives simultaneously. Contradicting yourself is a sign that you are brimming with possibilities.

'Only idiots fail to contradict themselves three times a day.'

Friedrich Nietzsche

Perfectionist? Plan to have more accidents on p. 110.
Lots to do? Pause for thoughtlessness on p. 107.

take jokes seriously

Many successful creative people don't start with grand visions of world domination but with a joke. When Mark Zuckerberg helped to create Facebook, he wasn't trying to build a global company; he was indulging in subversive humour. Facebook was developed to allow fellow students at Harvard to select the best-looking person from a choice of photos. It caused outrage and was banned by the college, but was so popular it crashed the university's servers.

Many of Andy Warhol's paintings started out as a joke. He produced a series of silkscreen paintings of dollar bills in rows and columns: a wry joke about the value of art. Collectors paid millions of dollars for a few dollars.

A joke that launched an artistic revolution was Marcel Duchamp's *Fountain*. It became one of the most influential works of the twentieth century. For a six-dollar fee, any artist could submit work to an exhibition held by the Society of Independent Artists. For a joke, Duchamp submitted a porcelain urinal that he'd bought from a New York plumbing supplier, signed it 'R. MUTT 1917' (the maker's name) and titled it *Fountain*. The piece was never exhibited; the curators refused to display it – but its submission caused uproar. Was it art or not? *Fountain* was thrown away. Forgotten. A photograph was the only record of the original object. The key to its success was that the photo was reproduced in an avant-garde art magazine with an accompanying article that eloquently explained the concept of the 'ready-made'. It started the ball rolling. The reputation of *Fountain* grew. It was repeatedly reproduced in art magazines and books. Collectors clamoured to buy it because of its fame, so Duchamp decided to remake it. There was a problem though; the manufacturer had stopped producing them. Duchamp had to hire craftsmen to make an exact replica from the photograph 'by hand' – a delicious irony.

Humour is a pattern-switching process. A joke is funny because it causes 'insight switchover' from a familiar pattern to a new, unexpected one. It is this moment of surprise and realisation that triggers laughter. Duchamp didn't intend *Fountain* to become the centrepiece for a history of modern art. He was poking fun at the Society of Independent Artists' reverence for traditional artistic skills. At that time the public had expectations that an artwork might be a bronze sculpture of female nudes or whatever, not a urinal. If Duchamp had thought *Fountain* was a masterpiece he wouldn't have thrown it away. It was only when the art world started taking the joke seriously that he too started taking it seriously. Spurred on by the unexpected success of *Fountain*, Duchamp started an art form known as the 'ready-made', an ordinary manufactured object that the artist selected and sometimes modified. Duchamp saw them as an antidote to traditional, handmade art. Simply by choosing the object, it became art.

The format of a conventional joke is that the listener is led down a familiar, 'reasonable' pathway. While they are travelling down this familiar road, the punchline suddenly shifts them onto a different, unexpected sidetrack. Creativity is about producing the unexpected and seeing things from a new perspective. Humour can be instrumental in shifting that expectation.

We often find ourselves feeling anxious, busy, harassed and trying to look productive at work. It's almost impossible to be inventive in that frame of mind. It hardly helps that our society believes that if you're having fun then you can't be getting the job done. Rather than being weighed down by a serious mindset, what we really need is humour. Humour is a key that opens the door to counter-intuitive and subversive thinking. If you have reached an impasse and are stuck with a problem, it can lead you to a fresh perspective and instigate insight or enlightenment.

'Only those who are capable of silliness can be called truly intelligent.'

Christopher Isherwood

Inspired? Be mature enough to be childish on p. 89.

look over the horizon

Some creative people are visionaries. Is it innate or a technique? 'It helps to see over the horizon,' said entrepreneur Ted Turner. Most people are too preoccupied with the present to look far ahead.

Why is Ted Turner regarded as a visionary entrepreneur? In the seventies Turner could see that the traditional nine to five working day was obsolete. Working hours were becoming more flexible. This was at odds with TV schedules; TV stations rigidly timetabled their news programmes for 6 and 10 p.m. Turner's idea was a twenty-four-hour news channel called CNN that anyone could dip into at any time. CNN covered worldwide news as it unfolded. Unlike the highly edited and smoothly presented mainstream channels, CNN was live, raw and immediate. Events like Poland's Solidarity strike, China's Tiananmen Square uprising and the 1991 Gulf War were beamed straight into living rooms. The reporters were breathless and unscripted. Ted Turner revolutionised news reporting and had a big hand in the creation of the 'global village'. CNN became the world's most widely internationally distributed news channel.

Turner read an article about communications satellites and realised he could use a satellite to reach the whole of North America and rival established TV stations. He was a visionary in the sense that he tried to work out what changes were coming in broadcasting and made sure he implemented them first.

After his father's suicide in 1963, Turner took over the small family billboard business, saved it from bankruptcy and turned it around. Turner applied his visionary process to the billboard advertising industry, the restaurant business, television and professional sports. He looked into their futures and then brought them into the present – each time creating multimillion-dollar businesses that enabled him to give over a billion dollars to charity.

'One morning, when Gregor Samsa woke from troubled dreams, he found himself transformed in his bed into a horrible vermin.' This is the opening sentence of Franz Kafka's classic *The Metamorphosis*, first published in 1915. Gregor finds himself suddenly transformed into a giant insect. He doesn't know how or why; he simply wakes up to find the world absurdly different – a classic Kafka scenario.

Kafka is considered a visionary writer who was years ahead of his time. His vision has evolved into an adjective, 'Kafkaesque', a term that describes a bleak world where people suffer trials for no reason and struggle with obscure authorities. Kafka worked as an insurance officer. He looked at the complicated bureaucracy he was a small part of and tried to predict where it would lead. His stories anticipate the rise of totalitarianism and the Holocaust. He could see the seeds of what was to come being planted around him and simply imagined it taken to an extreme.

Keith Haring was a visionary artist, whose imagery is an instantly recognisable visual language of the twentieth century. At the School of Visual Arts in New York in the early nineteen-eighties he studied drawing, painting, sculpture and art history. He developed a fluid use of line. His distinctive style was based on bold, graphic icons such as hearts, hands and a 'radiant baby' that were often merged with abstract patterns to create richly packed compositions.

Haring looked out for the seeds of the next important art movement, which had always emerged in the downtown galleries before moving uptown. He worked as an assistant in the Tony Shafrazi Gallery and gained an inside knowledge of the newest trends. The downtown galleries started to exhibit the graffiti artists who were blossoming on the streets and subway, but the work was formulaic – gaudy, multicoloured lettering. Every graffiti artist had the same style. Haring saw his chance. He aligned himself with the movement but his hard-edged black line and use of symbolic imagery stood out. He had a solo exhibition at the Tony Shafrazi Gallery and soon afterwards stepped into art history.

Visionaries do not literally have visions; they simply try to work out what the upcoming developments in their field are likely to be and implement them before anyone else. Most people are too busy myopically coping with day-to-day events to lift their heads up and look over the horizon.

'A visionary is someone who can see the future, or thinks he sees the future. In my case, I use it and it comes out right. That doesn't come from daydreams or dreams, but it comes from knowing the market and knowing the world and knowing people really well and knowing where they're going to be tomorrow.'

Leonard Lauder

Yes? Look into the future on p. 246.
No? Live in the here and now on p. 100.

go from A to B via Z

Lobsters hide in nooks and crannies in the rocks on the seabed. Sometimes they become wedged and can't move. They don't die because they draw food into their mouths by creating turbulence in the water with their claws. They literally grow into the rock. It's worth asking every now and then if this has happened to you.

I set my students at Central Saint Martins, the University of the Arts London, the task of finding a map of the area, drawing a circle round a glass on the map and then following it. They took it out onto the streets and followed the line without deviation. It took them to parts of the city they hadn't seen. They knocked on doors and persuaded the occupants to let them walk through their houses and offices. Sometimes I made it harder by asking the students to take a sofa along with them. It changed their perspective of the city. They met people they wouldn't normally meet, saw inside buildings that are normally closed to them. Other things they have done include staging football matches with three sides playing at the same time, and using a map of Paris to guide them around New York.

We all develop habits. We walk the same route to the subway, pick up the same paper and turn on the same computer – like robots. We find ourselves behaving automatically. We stop being aware of what we are doing, but to think creatively you have to be constantly aware. Awareness means that whatever you are doing you are in the moment and doing it with complete consciousness. Lack of awareness means that you are not alive to possibilities – you are missing opportunities.

Guy Debord pioneered a new way of perceiving the world called psychogeography. Its purpose was to jolt people into a new awareness of their surroundings. To wake them up. Psychogeographers devised situations that disrupted the ordinary and normal in order to shake people out of their customary ways of thinking and acting. The psycho-geographer finds different ways to travel and demands that you reconnect with the journey, to pretend you don't know your city, the roads or the buildings. We're prompted to look deeper, with fresh eyes, and act with heightened awareness.

One of my favourite examples of psychogeography was unintended. In *The Art of Looking Sideways*, Alan Fletcher tells of an American explorer who died at the North Pole. His relatives paid an Inuit a lot of money to fly back with the body. The Inuit had never before left the Arctic, so after he'd delivered the body he decided to spend the money travelling around the States. He didn't speak English though, so at railway stations, to buy a ticket he simply repeated, sound by sound, whatever the traveller standing in front of him said when they bought their ticket. The Inuit randomly crisscrossed the States. Eventually he ran out of money in a small town in Ohio. He lived there for the rest of his life.

If you always take the same path you will know where you are but you will lose yourself. If you always do the same things in the same way, you will get the same results. In any workplace it's easy to fall into the trap of doing the same old things in the same old way, and ending up with the same results. Change is good, even if it is just changing your desks around, or moving the photocopier. Growth is painful and change is painful, but nothing is more painful than staying in the wrong place. The more often you do something the same way, the more difficult it is to consider doing it differently. There are times when we all have to go from A to B – but go via Jupiter.

'Creativity is the defeat of habit by originality.'

Arthur Koestler

Discover what George Eliot had to say about repetition on p. 158.

immerse yourself

Ever had to solve a multidimensional jigsaw puzzle of egos and technical hitches in a fast-paced environment and not lose sight of your creative vision? It's possible if you use the right method.

I've stood next to a film director on a film set. I can't imagine a more stressful job. There was a constant stream of people asking, 'How should I light this?', 'How should I say this line?', 'Close up or long shot?'. They gave precise feedback to the cast and crew of grips, cameramen, lighting engineers, production designers, make-up artists . . . all the time keeping within budget. They started at 7 a.m. and usually put in a twenty-hour day in an atmosphere of total pandemonium. Add to that the pressure that if the film flops they may never make another. Sometimes they even write their own screenplays and edit or appear in their films.

The film director Peter Bogdanovich had answers to the barrage of questions because he could dip into his

---

encyclopaedic knowledge of film. He used index cards to record important data on and his personal assessment of every film he saw; between the ages of twelve and thirty he accumulated 5,316 of these cards. He went to six or eight movies a week. His favourites, like *Citizen Kane*, the film that inspired him to become a director, he saw multiple times. He got a job programming films for the Museum of Modern Art, then writing about films for *Esquire* magazine. When he interviewed directors they'd be impressed by his knowledge of their films. Bogdanovich could recite all the credits, recall each cut and camera move. They warmed to him and he became friends with the most famous directors of the time. He used to go to Times Square and watch five movies a day, then go home and watch more on *The Late Show*. At a film screening, a Hollywood hotshot who was impressed by his writing for *Esquire* offered him the role of assistant director on an upcoming movie. It went well and led to him directing his own movies. Whenever a problem arose on the set, he was able to draw on the formal and technical inspiration he had collected over years spent studying films.

His haunting film *The Last Picture Show* was nominated for eight Academy Awards in 1972. The film felt new and old at the same time because Bogdanovich shot in black and white when colour was standard. He used long tracking shots instead of breaking up important scenes, a result of studying *Citizen Kane* for hours. *The Last Picture Show* broke new ground by using a song score. Period-specific songs were played on radios, jukeboxes and gramophones within the film. It's been done to death since, but never with such subtlety.

It's a lesson in immersing yourself in every aspect of your interest. Know everything there is to know about it. Whether you work in finance, science, teaching or something else entirely, read every book and magazine, go to every lecture and research your subject in every way you can think of. When there is a crisis, you will have a pool of knowledge to dip into.

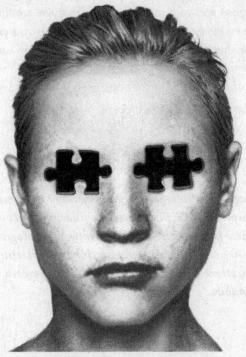

Quentin Tarantino was an employee of a video rental store called Video Archives. An obsessive film fan, he watched and discussed with the customers as many films as he could and paid close attention to the types of films they liked to rent. Tarantino has claimed that this influenced his decisions as a director; he has been quoted as saying: 'When people ask me if I went to film school, I tell them, "No, I went to films."' Both he and Bogdanovich taught themselves how to make films by studying films. Tarantino also used song scores, as Bogdanovich had.

Delve into books, magazines, documentaries, your culture, your heroes and your mentors, because these are the gateways to creative opportunities. They will open up a pathway to somewhere, maybe somewhere special. Be aware of the ideas circulating in your field. Certain ideas define the sensibilities of the culture at that one time. Make sure you are familiar with them.

'Nothing is original. Steal from anywhere that resonates with inspiration or fuels your imagination. Devour old films, new films, music, books, paintings, photographs, poems, dreams, random conversations, architecture, bridges, street signs, trees, clouds, bodies of water, light and shadows.'

Jim Jarmusch

Interested? Reinvent something that already exists on p. 198.
Not interested? Embrace ignorance on p. 128.

never leave improvisation to chance

When Herbie Hancock was playing with Miles Davis and hit some wrong chords, Miles Davis simply played a solo around them. Davis turned the bad notes into good music. He wasn't angry about the mistakes and didn't make Hancock feel bad about himself. The reason why Davis was so tolerant was because he was confident about his own abilities, confident he could handle anything thrown at him. This in turn made Hancock feel confident and free to experiment. An improvisational attitude encourages people to be flexible and adapt.

Miles Davis's group made quick decisions under pressure. All jazz musicians improvise when soloing, but Davis created an atmosphere in which his musicians never censured one another's mistakes – errors were simply a more unusual route. He would often discourage them from practising a tune before recording it in order to encourage them to take risks and try new possibilities – a fresh discovery could always be waiting around the corner. This is why, when Davis's band performed, they sounded way better than the sum of their parts.

Miles Davis's leadership shows us the benefit of adapting to complexity and constant change at work. His band negotiated with one another as they played; they didn't dwell on mistakes or stifle one another's ideas. This improvisational 'jazz mindset' is essential for effective leadership.

New and challenging situations often require us to take up the art of improvisation. As such, a jazz band is the perfect model of how any big company or organisation should function. Organisations generally follow the old-fashioned hierarchical model whereby management is about planning, organising and controlling. Leaders are seen as conductors in charge of an orchestra following a rigid script. People are judged by how closely they follow the script. This instills a fear of getting things wrong, of making mistakes. The world champion boxer Mike Tyson said, 'Everyone has a plan until they get punched in the mouth.' Most plans get punched in the mouth. Confident leaders see a mistake as an invitation to a new route. They organise themselves so that they can be at their best, whatever happens.

It's a mistake not to make mistakes. Like Miles Davis, leaders need to master the art of experimentation and take turns soloing. The world's best leaders and teams improvise. Jazz shows that organisations must take an inventive approach to management and economic volatility. Improvisation is too important to leave to chance.

'More of me comes out when I improvise.'

Edward Hopper

Inspired? Plan to have more accidents on p. 110.

reject acceptance
and accept rejection

Here are some famous books and the number of times they were rejected by publishers before finally being published. *Jonathan Livingston Seagull* by Richard Bach was rejected 140 times, *Gone With the Wind* by Margaret Mitchell thirty-eight, *Carrie* by Stephen King thirty, *Watership Down* by Richard Adams twenty-six, *Harry Potter and the Philosopher's Stone* by J.K. Rowling twelve, *Twilight* by Stephenie Meyer fourteen.

What these writers all had in common was a discipline and dedication to sacrifice comfort, to see their projects through. Every time a manuscript was rejected they reworked it, improved the opening line, made the opening paragraph more dynamic or added a more dramatic ending. They improved their work and they improved as writers. Overcoming the adversity of rejection opened up avenues of personal discovery that enabled them to uncover the nature of their true selves.

No one likes rejection. The small consolation with criticism is that at least someone is taking you seriously, whereas rejection means that they just don't care. All the great creative thinkers have experienced this. Their response determined whether they would ultimately be a success or failure. Rejection strengthens and invigorates the resolve of highly successful people.

Fear of rejection can stop you from putting your work out there. Those rejecting you – art dealers, publishers, promoters or collectors – have their own motivations. When a gallery turns an artist's work away it's often not because the work is poor quality, but because it doesn't suit the philosophy of the gallery or the style or subject matter isn't compatible with their other artists'. Perhaps the prices for the work are too high or too low for their collectors. Maybe it's simply too large for the gallery. It's not always a judgement about whether it's good or bad.

Great creative people work out that they have nothing to lose by rejection. It is their dreams for the future that have been turned down, not their present reality. They hope to get their paintings exhibited in a top gallery. If they try and fail they'll just be in the same situation, not any worse off. They have nothing to lose by trying, so they try and try again.

I once bumped into one of my ex-students, who optimistically said, 'My rejection letters have been more encouraging lately.' I'll never forget his positive attitude. It was really touching. Later still I heard he'd had an acceptance letter. Praise and success breeds complacency and mediocrity. Rejection breeds determination. It encourages you to re-examine your work and improve it, to strive to be better.

'I think all great innovations are built on rejections.'

Louis-Ferdinand Céline

Discover the joy of self-doubt and inadequacy on p. 43.

be as annoying as possible

In 1729 Jonathan Swift wrote and published a book, *A Modest Proposal*, that suggested poor children should be eaten. Swift was a respected writer of books such as *Gulliver's Travels* and, when he suggested in his new book that Irish parents should sell their children to the rich as food, it was by some taken seriously. The book describes the plight of starving beggars in Ireland and proceeds to observe, 'A young healthy child well nursed, is, at a year old, a most delicious, nourishing and wholesome food, whether stewed, roasted, baked or boiled.' Swift explained in detail why it is a good idea to eat children; he listed recipes, preparation methods for cooking and calculations explaining the financial benefits to the poor. Readers thought Swift was seriously suggesting cannibalism and infanticide. They were outraged. Towards the end of the book Swift gradually introduced the reforms he claimed to believe were the solution and the reader slowly realised they had been provoked.

Swift's book had a profound impact. A sober and conventional proposal of reforms could have gone unnoticed. Swift wanted something to happen. He wanted to change things quickly. He needed to make an impact and to get his point across to the maximum amount of people. He took a chance. He walked along the edge of a precipice. It could have backfired badly, but it didn't.

Being provocative is a legitimate tactic. Provoke a reaction. Provoke change. Provoke awareness. It's important to get people emotionally involved. If you have a message you want to communicate, you need to attract people's attention. Otherwise you're talking to yourself. Every creative thinker is at heart a cultural provocateur who wants to change, transform and raise awareness.

Creativity is not for the cautious. It's for people who put their neck on the line. Sometimes we need to provoke a reaction in people. We should not be scared of causing offence; we should be scared of not being heard.

'I obviously irritate people. I obviously antagonise them.'

Peter Greenaway

Inspired? Throw truth bombs on p. 144.

cross-pollinate

Most of you are alive to read this thanks to Alexander Fleming. Millions of lives have been saved by his discovery of penicillin and antibiotics. If an antibiotic hasn't saved you personally, it has saved one of your ancestors.

What distinguished Fleming from other scientists was that he thought like an artist; he was more interested in experiments that went wrong than those that worked. He didn't follow the logical and reasonable path but searched instead for the weird and different. He favoured the methods of artists over those of scientists.

In September 1928, Fleming found a fungus killing abandoned bacterial cultures. He was fascinated by the colours and patterns they created. This led to Fleming discovering the antibiotic properties of penicillin, properties that would change the world of medicine for ever. Many other scientists had seen penicillin growing on their Petri dishes before Fleming, but they had dismissed them as mistakes and thrown them away.

Fleming was a keen watercolour painter. He had more affinity with the artists he mixed with at the Chelsea Arts Club than with his fellow scientists. He also painted in unusual mediums, depicting dancers, buildings, battle scenes and other subjects using bacteria. He created these paintings by growing microbes in Petri dishes filled with agar, a gelatin-like substance, applying different species to different areas according to the colour he knew they would grow as. The colours of the bacteria paintings were vibrant. The reality that they were alive added to Fleming's excitement. Fleming's palette grew richer as he continued to discover bacteria with suitable pigments. He collected bacteria for their artistic qualities while other scientists only collected what was useful or practical.

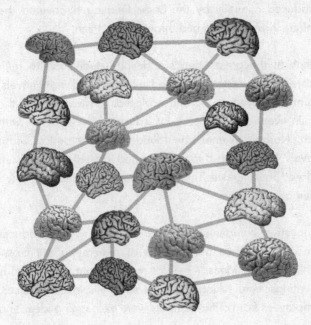

Fleming was as much an artist as a scientist and blurred the lines between the two disciplines. His lab was as messy as an artist's studio. Petri dishes, microbes and scientific equipment were scattered randomly about. When Fleming discovered penicillin, what he had really been looking for was something he could use in one of his paintings, something rare. Fleming spent his life searching for the unusual and the processes that created them.

Fleming made other discoveries as he searched for the strange and unusual. Once, he let mucus drip from his nose onto a Petri dish just to see what would happen. A new colour? A new bacterium? He found that his mucus killed bacteria. He had discovered lysozyme, an antibiotic produced naturally by the body. Fleming discovered the unique in what others had thrown in the trash.

Many of the great scientists, despite dedication to their subject, were deeply interested in the arts and wrote novels, painted, played music and sculpted. Einstein played the violin every day, and took his instrument everywhere with him. Norbert Wiener, the founder of cybernetics, wrote novels. Darwin was deeply interested in Shelley. Niels Bohr adored Shakespeare. Their broad interest in culture enriched their own subjects.

Innovative companies like Danish hearing-aid producer Oticon appreciate the benefits of generating the cross-pollination of ideas. They discovered that spontaneous meetings were taking place on stairwells in their offices. Employees from different floors were exchanging ideas and information. Oticon widened the stairs to encourage these multidisciplinary discussions. Nokia encouraged their staff to eat lunch in their cafeterias and not to eat at their desk or go out. Their employees mixed with people from diverse departments and it was a valuable way of cross-pollinating ideas. Successful creative thinkers search for ideas from any source.

'You can look anywhere and find inspiration.'

Frank Gehry

Find out how Robert Zimmerman used a similar approach to turn himself into the world's most popular singer-songwriter on p. 161. Or meet another great thinker who refused to be constrained by the limits of his field – and made us all richer in the process on p. 55.

stay playful

Out of the blue the Fox Broadcasting Company asked Matt Groening to pitch to create a short animation for TV. It was his big break. Groening intended to use the characters from his successful cartoon strip, 'Life in Hell'. He discovered fifteen minutes before the pitch that Fox would insist on owning all rights to the characters, and didn't want to lose control of them. He decided not to show them what he had prepared and needed a completely new idea, immediately. In a desperate situation, Groening hurriedly formulated the dysfunctional cartoon family The Simpsons while waiting in the lobby. He gave them the only names he could think of quickly, those of his own parents and siblings. He won the pitch. It evolved into a half-hour programme running every week for more than twenty years – generating movies, books, toys and a pop culture empire worth millions. There has never been a TV show to equal its cultural impact.

Mindlessly memorising old information at school was so boring to Matt Groening that he was completely disengaged. He wanted to express himself so during his lessons he secretly drew instead. The thrill of making something out of nothing inspired him to produce hundreds of drawings. His refuge was the art room. He soon realised he lacked traditional artistic talent, so he incorporated stories and jokes into his drawings to make them more interesting. He explained that cartooning suited people like him who couldn't quite draw and couldn't quite write – so they had to put those two half-talents together to come up with a career. Groening believed cartoons would be his livelihood. His friends had similar dreams too, but one by one they became serious grown-ups. Groening knew he couldn't follow them. He continued to play; he worked as a cartoonist and did part-time jobs to stay afloat financially.

Groening watched the spirits of his contemporaries, who had taken a serious attitude to their professions, slowly wither and die. Their lives dried up as his blossomed.

Whoever you are or whatever you do, staying playful is the only way to make the most of the situation. Play can help any field of activity, because through it we discover and explore all available options.

Author and psychiatrist Dr Stuart Brown spent decades studying the importance of play for people in all walks of life, including business people and Nobel Prize winners. He reviewed over 6,000 case studies that explored the role of play in each person's life. He discovered that lack of play was an important factor in predicting criminal behaviour among murderers in Texas prisons. Brown explained that play should be 'purposeless, fun and pleasurable'. The focus should be on the actual experience, not on achieving a reward. Unfortunately the only kind of play acceptable to society is competitive play, usually sports that have a clear goal of victory.

Play is a catalyst. It boosts productivity and is vital for problem-solving. Play is not taken seriously enough; it is as important for adults as for children. We don't lose the need for novelty just because we become older. We all need to remember that play creates useful and practical solutions. You're a success in your field if you don't know whether what you're doing is work or play.

'Man is most nearly himself when he achieves the seriousness of a child at play.'

Heraclitus

Feeling too old to be childish? *Let Georgia O'Keeffe persuade you otherwise on p. 63.*

don't be recessive in a recession

The Kellogg's company was transformed into a success by a counter-intuitive decision by Will Keith Kellogg. In the late nineteen-twenties, Kellogg's was one of the companies competing in the market for packaged cereal. When the Depression struck, the other companies did the predictable thing: they reined in expenses and cut back on advertising. All the big companies reduced their expenditure. Recessions are a time when short-term considerations beat long-term potential.

The major companies looked around at each other and thought, 'They're cutting their budget – we'd better do the same.' It was the accepted wisdom. In hard times most firms invest less in research and development. They try to preserve what they have. That was rational. It made sense. Kellogg made an irrational decision: he doubled the advertising budget. Kellogg did the opposite of everyone else. He thought things through for himself. The Great Depression was beginning, but he reasoned that people still needed to eat and the breakfast of choice for most

Americans was 'flakes and milk'. That was what distinguished him as a creative thinker, rather than just another CEO. Kellogg listened to a host of financial experts. His accountants and financial advisers were pressuring him to make cuts, but sometimes the clamour of experts creates clouds of confusion and it takes an original thinker to see with clarity.

Recessions create more opportunity for challenges, not less. Kellogg saw that he would never have such a huge competitive advantage again. When everyone is spending freely on advertising, it's difficult to stand out from the pack. But when ads are scarcer, the returns on the outlay rise. Decades later, statistics still show that companies that continue spending on advertising during recessions do significantly better than those which make big cuts. So what happens? Companies continue to cut advertising in recessions. Their instinct is to cut back. Spending in a recession seems wrong, even though it's right. At the beginning of the Depression Kellogg's had been vying for dominance in the cereal market. By the end, it totally dominated the market.

Our heads are full of ideas that we have inherited from our culture, families and institutions. We receive them when we are young and open to the concepts being pressed on to us. They are part of our social conditioning. Original thinkers are able to put these received ideas aside. They analyse *how* they are thinking as well as *what* they are thinking. This enables them to see these accepted truths for what they are, and to go along with them or ignore them as they see fit.

Try to put a distance between yourself and the common wisdom. If you clarify your thoughts, you'll have a deeper understanding than those around you. Be prepared to swim against the tide.

'The biggest competitive advantage is to do the right thing at the worst time.'

Bill Hewlett and David Packard

Meet three other luminaries who swam against the tide on p. 55, p. 235 and p. 267.

project yourself into the future

Torrential rain hammers down from permanently dark skies onto a sprawling city of glass and steel. In the decaying streets, all traces of nature have been obliterated. Overhead, flying cars soar between the buildings and a huge hovering airship projects adverts for 'adventure' in Off-world locations. Thunderous sounds rumble as belching mushroom clouds of fire and smoke randomly erupt. Most people have left the planet for an Off-world colony, driven away by crime and pollution. A mixture of races mingle in the retrofitted bars, where amidst the chaos and destruction the camera falls on a Blade Runner.

Ridley Scott's film *Blade Runner* imagines the implications of cloning and creating artificial human beings; of a paranoid world where searchlights penetrate into every dark corner and the police are omnipresent; of the unchecked growth of corporate power as the Tyrell Corporation looms over the city in a giant pyramid. Science fiction asks the question, 'Will the future be a utopia or a dystopia?' An ideal society where everyone lives in harmony or an entirely dysfunctional society?

The Chinese lacked the ability to imagine anything new or see into the future. They were world leaders in manufacturing – but they needed someone to tell them what to manufacture. They couldn't invent their own products. The Chinese government wanted to change that, so they sent a delegation to the USA to research how the workforce at Apple, Google and Microsoft became so innovative. They questioned them in an attempt to find out where their creativity and inventiveness came from. Apple and Google were inventing the future for themselves and for the rest of us – but how did they do it? The researchers found one common factor – most of them had been fans of science-fiction books when they were young.

Science fiction is a combination of rigorous science and unfettered imagination. Fantasy is important to the development of science. Fiction enables you to fly without leaving the ground. Science-fiction cities and cars eventually become the real cities and cars we live in and drive. Fiction takes you to places you've never been and places that don't exist. Once you've visited the future, you are less content with the world around you. That discontent drives people to alter and improve, to make things better.

The Chinese had a problem, though: they had banned science fiction. During the Anti-Spiritual Pollution Campaign (1983–1984) the government labelled science fiction as 'spiritual pollution'. They couldn't see any practical benefit in it, and they didn't want people to be imaginative or come up with new ideas; it is in the nature of new ideas that they are subversive. As a result of their research in the USA, though, the Chinese switched from banning science fiction to vigorously promoting it. China is now the world's biggest market for science fiction with the highest circulation of magazines and books.

Silicon Valley is the nickname for an area of San Francisco that was and is home to many of the world's largest technology corporations. What distinguishes these companies is that they are more interested in the future than the past or present. They are always looking forward. The structure of the companies is fluid and flexible so that they can change and adapt quickly. A feature of Google, Apple, eBay, Yahoo and many others is that they are fascinated by the future. They constantly try to anticipate, predict and shape what's coming.

You create science fiction. We all do: we plan new kitchens, careers and holidays. We see ourselves in them. We visualise them. What would the best and worst be like? We see the events, hear the sounds and feel the emotions.

The ability to project ourselves into the future is one of the key features of being human. Our imaginations are the most powerful tools we have, more powerful than any car, aeroplane or rocket because it's our imaginations that create the car, aeroplane and rocket. Imagination has practical benefits – but it needs to be constantly maintained or it rusts and falls apart. Where are you going? To what extent can you shape your own destiny? Any one of us, at any time, can change our route by asking, 'Who do I want to be in ten years?', 'Where do I want to be in ten years?' or 'What do I want to be doing?'

'Change is the law of life. And those who look only to the past or present are certain to miss the future.'

John F. Kennedy

Not sure? Try living in the here and now instead on p. 100.

get out of your mind

Insane women in a lunatic asylum made Hans Christian Andersen realise he was too sane.

Andersen achieved worldwide fame in the nineteenth century for his imaginative and exotic fairy tales such as 'The Ugly Duckling' and 'The Princess and the Pea', which remain classics. His stories continue to be read across the world. They have introduced generations of children to a whimsical world of imagination. Andersen crafted tales and built dreamy, fantastical worlds that were driven by an intuitive common sense.

Tales told by women who had been committed to the local lunatic asylum, where his grandmother was a gardener, inspired him. Andersen sat and listened avidly to their improvised tales full of witches, fairies, goblins and trolls. They schooled him in the art of stream of consciousness and improvised storytelling. Imaginative worlds, strange surreal characters and weird situations poured from their unbalanced minds. As Ray Charles put it, 'Dreams, if they're any good, are always a little bit crazy.' But their stories were without form; Andersen combined their exotic imaginations with structured plots. Getting those twin aspects working in tandem was the key to his success.

He combined the absurd and irrational with his literary skill, gripping plotlines and perceptive observations of human behaviour. Andersen's bizarre characters look at the world with a distorted perspective and are unable to see or understand their real situation. Many credit Andersen with exploring the subconscious mind decades before Freud's studies and see him as a forerunner to the twentieth century's surrealist movement.

Creativity requires a mixture of unfettered imagination and practical application; random invention and playfulness, held together with an underlying thread. Children and the insane are great examples of how to think in an unfettered and unconstrained way. Their thoughts flow freely and are always flexible and random. Doors to unexplored areas constantly open up for them. But children and the insane don't drive technological, creative and artistic innovation; they lack the organisational skills. Creative thinking requires a balance of each.

Imagination and fantasy are essential components of a healthy, satisfying mental life. Unfettered imagination has positive and useful results in our daily lives. Imagination enables us to rehearse and constructively plan. Try to encourage your mind to wander – it will produce tangible results. Forgetting a practical task because your attention has drifted is of little consequence if that daydream has enabled you to access a key insight.

'Open the window of fantasy to know what reality can bring.'

Raul D. Arellano

Discover why the author hasn't done any ironing for two years – and why that's a good thing – on p. 173.

box your way out of boxes

Asked to write an extremely short story for a magazine? Make a feature of the brevity. Asked to design a building on a steep mountainside? Build out in a way that exaggerates the acute angles. Asked to paint a picture on a curved ceiling split into sections? Michelangelo overcame these limitations when painting the ceiling of the Sistine Chapel. The biggest challenge was fitting human figures into a ceiling criss-crossed by spandrels. The chapel ceiling was a barrel vault, curving downwards, segregated by spandrels and viewed from sixty feet below. It required amazing imagination to adapt to the perspective distortion. Michelangelo used the unusual shapes of the spandrels to create a more dynamic composition than if he had been given the freedom of a clear ceiling. He had to design scaffolding built out from holes in the wall rather than built up from the floor. For the first time in his career he had to use the complicated fresco painting technique. He painted standing and looking upwards for months, making it the most physically demanding painting ever completed. The expanse was huge in comparison to other great paintings: roughly 12,000 square feet.

Five hundred years later, the ceiling still inspires awe. It's a masterpiece of drama, colour, people, motion and scenes. The viewer hardly notices the spandrels because they are so well integrated into the composition.

Sometimes we feel boxed in by restrictions, but we must make the most of the limitations imposed on us and search for ways around, under and over barriers. Restrictions force the inventive into unique and unusual solutions. Don't dismiss an opportunity that's outside your usual area. Practical difficulties can lead to original solutions. Creativity requires mental liberation; it needs to be liberated from something, which means it needs barriers to overcome. Creativity is often a response to constraint.

'In art, progress lies not in an extension, but in a knowledge of limitations.'

Georges Braque

More? Make freedom a career on p. 270, or discover how to turn a setback into an opportunity on p. 141.

to learn, teach

I was taught by one of the most famous artists of all time, the Renaissance master Raphael. There is a direct line of teaching that leads from Raphael to me. I discovered this via a piece of work by the fascinating English artist Tom Phillips; he traced back his artistic connections and I have adapted his findings to my own lineage. When I was at university I was taught by one of England's greatest modern artists, Frank Auerbach, who was taught by David Bomberg; he in turn was taught by the great English Impressionist, Walter Sickert. Then an unbroken teaching line flows through famous Romantic artists and French portrait painters, via Degas back to Ingres and Primaticcio, Giulio Romano and culminates in the Renaissance with Raphael. It's possible to go back even further – Raphael was taught by Giovanni Santi, then Pietro Perugino and on and on. Now I am a tutor at Central Saint Martins, not so much because I want to teach but because I want to learn from my students. I leave at the end of the day inspired and brimming with new ideas.

So what? A way of thinking was passed on. They were all passionate about the hard truth that teaching is about indicating the right questions, not giving the right answers. Real magic occurs when everyone learns together and is simultaneously teacher and student.

The great German composer Carl Orff composed one of the most famous works of the twentieth century, the awesome *Carmina Burana*. But Orff made a greater contribution to music through teaching. He developed a method, the Orff Schulwerk, which used imitation, exploration, improvisation and composition in lessons similar to a child's world of play. It has arguably touched more lives than all the classical music of the twentieth century together.

Many famous artists, writers, composers and scientists teach. Not for the money but to keep in touch with the young and with new ideas being generated in their field. 'While we teach, we learn,' said Roman philosopher Seneca. The best way to understand a concept is to explain it to someone else.

The true teacher protects students against their influence. They inspire students to distrust them. They produce no disciples. A creative teacher teaches nothing but provides a learning environment. Their main task is to teach students to question everything – including their teacher.

'You cannot teach a man anything, you can only help him find it within himself.'

Galileo

Discover why even teachers shouldn't be experts on p. 50.

be an everyday radical

Medical intern Barry Marshall's colleagues watched in horror. He had taken some bacteria from the gut of a patient seriously ill with a stomach ulcer and poured the murky brown soup into a glass. Then he drank it. The potion contained over a billion *Helicobacter pylori* bacteria and tasted like swamp water.

A few days later, Marshall started suffering from nausea and vomiting. An endoscopy proved that his stomach had gone from being pink and healthy to red and massively inflamed, the early stages of a stomach ulcer. In 1984 there was no cure, but Marshall took antibiotics and miraculously healed himself. He had proved that stomach ulcers were caused by bacteria, reversing decades of medical doctrine that they were caused by stress and too much acid. The significance was enormous: if ulcers were caused by bacteria they could be cured. It was one of the great breakthroughs in medical history, saved millions of lives and won Marshall a Nobel Prize.

Marshall had taken two safety precautions: he didn't inform the hospital ethics committee because they were certain to refuse permission. Committees and creativity don't mix. He didn't tell his wife because spouses are always overcautious on each other's behalf. She guessed within a few days anyway, when he began vomiting and his breath smelled putrid.

Marshall was driven to do it because, although he had already proved their case through studies of their patients, mainstream doctors were dismissive. They clung to the established dogma that ulcers, which at that time affected ten per cent of all adults, were caused by stress. Marshall had to watch in horror as ulcer patients had their stomachs removed or bled until they died.

The innate snobbery of the medical profession meant that innovation had to come from the established research medical centres, not the Australian outback. Marshall was a thirty-three-year-old intern, not even a proper doctor. A researcher who attended one of his presentations commented, 'He simply didn't have the demeanour of a scientist.' Marshall had also pitched himself against pharma-ceutical companies that had invested millions in products that alleviated the symptoms without curing them. The new theory would throw all that profit out of the window. Marshall said, 'Everyone was against me, but I knew I was right.'

Marshall was unable to prove his case in experiments on animals because Helicobacter pylori only affected primates. Banned from experimenting on people, Marshall was desperate so he experimented on the only volunteer around: himself.

To act radically in the face of elite hierarchies and accepted practices is creative. It was essential for Beethoven as an artist to fight against the status quo. He battled against the standardisation of musical forms by reinventing the structure and scope of symphonies, string quartets, concertos and sonatas. At that time composers were paid servants, but Beethoven changed that. He demanded and received high fees. He was the first musician to dine with his patrons rather than the servants – and it didn't stop him being an unsociable and argumentative dinner guest. CEOs used to take over a company and steady the ship. Now they upset the status quo, set up a new team and bring in new ideas. If you want to transform things you need to be in a radical frame of mind.

'Any behavior that is not the status quo is interpreted as insanity, when, in fact, it might actually be enlightenment. Insanity is sorta in the eye of the beholder.'

Chuck Palahniuk

Discover another medical breakthrough that wouldn't have happened without upsetting the status quo on p. 158.

make freedom a career

Dr Seuss's editors bet him he couldn't write a book with a limit of only fifty different words. Dr Seuss won the bet and in the process produced one of the highest-selling children's books of all time, *Green Eggs and Ham*. Van Gogh used a maximum of six colours when painting. Picasso focused on one colour during his Blue Period. They imposed these limitations on themselves. They needed a framework, but it was their framework, one that suited them.

Jackson Pollock's paintings may look chaotic but they are highly organised. He planned the colour scheme for each one in advance, usually no more than eight to ten colours. He used industrial paint so the colours were ready-mixed in large tins before he started the work. Paint lends itself to hundreds of mark-making techniques: scumbles, glazes, dabs, scrapes – thousands of possibilities. But Pollock only used one technique, dribbles. He used no figurative imagery. He defined clear limits for his work and kept rigidly to them. But within them he worked with freedom. He didn't make rules; they were more like compass points for him to keep his bearings, to prevent him getting lost in a myriad of possibilities. In the nineteen-fifties art critics hailed Pollock's huge abstract expressionist paintings as revolutionary and unique.

If you have to decide between a good choice and a bad choice, it's easy. When you have to decide between a good choice, a good choice or another good choice, it's hard. Psychologists have uncovered the fact that too many choices, even between good options, lead to decision paralysis. Professor Hazel Rose Markus of Stanford

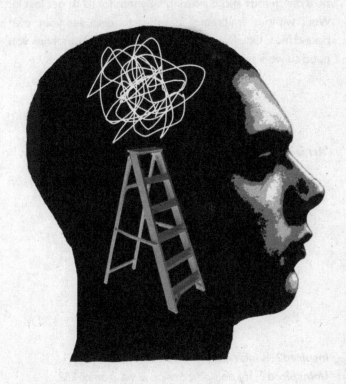

University's Department of Psychology says: 'Even in contexts where choice can foster freedom, empowerment, and independence, it is not an unalloyed good. Choice can also produce a numbing uncertainty, depression, and selfishness.'

If you work without boundaries, you'll discover what boundaries you need to erect for yourself. Creative people need to work with complete freedom but, paradoxically, to prevent themselves descending into chaos they set parameters and limitations within which they work. Complete freedom can be a dangerous and confusing labyrinth for us to get lost in. Work without limitations in order to discover your own boundaries. Once you have worked out the boundaries you need to work within, you can work with freedom.

'Art is limitation; the essence of every picture is the frame.'

G.K. Chesterton

Inspired? Bring chaos to order on p. 192.
Uninspired? Try going from A to B via Z on p. 232.

exercises

The following exercises are not designed to produce specific results but to stimulate you.

They refer to many of the creative people we've looked at in the book.

Pick a fight with yourself

For one day, contradict yourself. If you usually get up late, get up early. Ask yourself, 'Why do I do things this way?' If you 'can't live' without a morning coffee, have orange juice instead. Question the things you do unquestioningly. If you normally work at the computer, work on paper instead. When you are working, work in the opposite way. Be contrary with yourself, all day. Do the opposite of what you want to do. Rewiring your circuitry will give you a deeper understanding of yourself.

Think about your thinking

Analyse the way you think. What was your best idea? Think back to how you had it and what preceded it. What was your stupidest idea? Did it germinate in a different way to your best idea? Who regularly inspires you? What can you learn from them? What do you enjoy most about your working process? Produce a diagram of your thought processes. Make it practical and down to earth, like drawing a diagram of the workings of a car engine. Then study it. Any surprises?

Be alone with 'friends'

It's quite hard to be creative without being solitary now and then. The creative people I've known who work a lot with people – choreographers, theatre directors, company directors – all need a surprisingly high amount of solitude. Space to think. Sit in a room and let your thoughts wander. Start with a minute, and then build up to ten, then longer. This is the opposite of meditating: you're not trying to empty your mind of thoughts; you're trying to fill it up with thoughts. Ideas will start to creep into your mind. Now you're not alone, you have friends. Develop them.

Look at the overlooked

Many of the creative people we've looked at have been observant. They've been attentive and noticed something others have missed. While playing with his children in a playground, Walt Disney noticed how many bored parents there were sitting around. 'Why isn't there any entertainment here for the parents?' he wondered. He had the idea for Disneyland. Go into a public space and write down twenty observations of people. Study them. Try to understand them.

Rename yourself

Mozart renamed himself almost every week, all his life. He was baptised Joannes Chrysostomus Wolfgangus Theophilus Mozart but he generally referred to himself as Amade. When he married, he changed his name to Adam, the first man, as a way to declare himself reborn. He constantly altered his name as a way to experiment with different identities. Think of ten new names for yourself. Are they a statement of your beliefs? What do they tell people about you?

The object of the object

Gather together a few objects, maybe a pair of scissors, a roll of tape, a stapler – anything. Now play with possible combinations. Move them around. See how they might fit together. Eventually they will form a combination that seems right or feels inevitable. You may have invented a new tool, or a work of art. It will reveal to you how you think about things.

Overhear over there

The film director Christopher Guest gets ideas by listening to people. While waiting in a hotel lobby he overheard an inane conversation between members of a second-rate rock band, and the film *This is Spinal Tap* was born. Sit in a café, bar or on a bus and write down conversations you overhear. You'll be surprised at the extraordinary nuggets that will emerge.

Make a mark

Sometimes one of my students is burning with the desire to be creative, but doesn't know how to start. It may be that they love painting and desperately want to paint, but can't think *what* to paint. They are waiting for a deeply meaningful, earth-shattering concept. It never arrives. I get them to make a mark on a canvas with paint. It might be a slashing stroke. Then make another mark in response. Then another. A conversation begins. Soon they have a painting. The same is true of writing or any field of creativity. Write one word, then another in response. Soon you'll have a story.

references

Biskind, Peter, 1998. Easy Riders, Raging Bulls. USA: Simon and Schuster.

Branson, Richard, 2012. Richard Branson Bares His Business 'Secrets'. http://www.npr.org/2012/10/10/162587389/virgins-richard-branson-bares-his-business-secrets

Buckminster Fuller, R. http//www.designmuseum.org/design/r-buckminster-fuller

Csikszentmihalyi, Mihaly, 1996. Creativity. USA: HarperCollins.

Dalí, Salvador. http://www.youtube.com/watch?v=Wj9YAib_Xnl

Dash, Joan, 2000. The Longitude Prize. USA: FSG.

De La Roca, Claudia, 2012. Matt Groening Reveals the Location of the Real Springfield. http://www.smithsonian-mag.com/arts-culture/matt-groening-reveals-the-location-of-the-real-springfield-60583379/?no-ist

Dunn, Rob, 2010. Painting With Penicillin: Alexander Fleming's Germ Art. http://www.smithsonianmag.com/science-nature/painting-with-penicillin-alexander-flemings-germ-art-1761496/?no-ist

Feynman, Richard, 1994. No Ordinary Genius: The Illustrated Richard Feynman. New York: W.W. Norton & Company, Inc.

Finch, Christopher, 2010. Chuck Close: Life. USA, Prestel.

Gaiman, Neil, 2013. Reading and Obligation. http://readingagency.org.uk/news/blog/neil-gaiman-lecture-in-full.html

Kathleen D. Vohs, Joseph P. Redden, and Ryan Rahinel, 2013. Physical Order Produces Healthy Choices, Generosity, and Conventionality, Whereas Disorder Produces Creativity. Carlson School of Management, University of Minnesota.

Klotz, Laurence, November 2005. How (Not) to Communicate New Scientific Information: A Memoir of the Famous Brindley Lecture. BJU International.

Marshall, Barry J., 2005. Helicobacter Connections. http://www.nobelprize.org/nobel_prizes/medicine/laureates/2005/marshall-lecture.pdf

McNeal, Jeff, 1999. A candid conversation with Pixar. http://www.thebigpicturedvd.net/bigreport4.shtml

Morais, Fernando, 2010. Paulo Coelho: A Warrior's Life – The Authorized Biography. England: HarperOne.

Ordóñez, Lisa D., Maurice E. Schweitzer, Adam D. Galinsky, and Max H. Bazerman, 2009. Goals Gone Wild: The Systematic Side Effects of Over-Prescribing Goal Setting. Harvard Business School.

Orenstein, Arbie (ed.), 2003. A Ravel Reader: Correspondence, Articles, Interviews. London, Dover Publications.

Ponseti, Ignacio. http://www.ponseti.info/clubfoot-and-the-ponseti-method/what-is-clubfoot/ponseti-method.html

Roylance, Brian (ed.), 2000. The Beatles Anthology. England, Weidenfeld & Nicolson.

Samuelson, Paul A., 1970. How I Became an Economist. http://www.nobelprize.org/nobel_prizes/economic-sciences/laureates/1970/samuelson-article2.html

Tharp, Twyla, 2002. The Creative Habit: Learn It and Use it for Life. London, Simon and Schuster.

Tim Rees, Jessica Salvatore, Pete Coffee, S. Alexander Haslam, Anne Sargent, Tom Dobson, 2013. Reversing downward performance spirals, Journal of Experimental Social Psychology, Volume 49, Issue 3, pages 400–403.

Tufte, Edward, 1997. Visual Explanations: Images and Quantities, Evidence and Narrative. USA: Graphics Press.

Usher, Shaun, 2014. Letters of Note: An Eclectic Collection of Correspondence Deserving a Wider Audience. USA, Chronicle Books.

Winslet, Kate. The impostor phenomenon – Feeling like a fraud, 2000. http://theinneractor.com/111/feeling-like-a-fraud/

acknowledgements

Thanks to my daughter Scarlet Judkins for modelling for the illustration in Get Out of Your Mind, Be a Conservative Revolutionary, and Design a Difference. To my son Louis Judkins for modelling in, Make Freedom a Career, Make What You Say Unforgettable, Open Your Mind and for using his hands and various body parts in other illustrations. The ball of energy and inspiration that is Zelda Malan suggested numerous improvements. Thanks to Drummond Moir for commissioning and editing the book and his inventive suggestions and contributions. Without my literary agent, Jonathan Conway, the book would never have got off the ground. Thanks to Jacqui Lewis for copy-editing and Barbara Roby for proofreading. The eye-catching cover was designed by Ben Summers. Thanks to my colleagues and students at the universities where I teach.

Join a literary community of
like-minded readers who seek out
the best in contemporary writing.

From the thousands of submissions Sceptre
receives each year, our editors select the books
we consider to be outstanding.

We look for distinctive voices, thought-provoking
themes, original ideas, absorbing narratives and
writing of prize-winning quality.

If you want to be the first to hear about our
new discoveries, and would like the chance to
receive advance reading copies of our books
before they are published, visit

www.sceptrebooks.co.uk

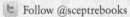 Follow @sceptrebooks

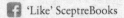 'Like' SceptreBooks

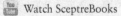 Watch SceptreBooks